Phillip D. Jensen

1 & 2 Timothy

Guard the Gospel

GOOD BOOK GUIDE

7-Session Bible Study

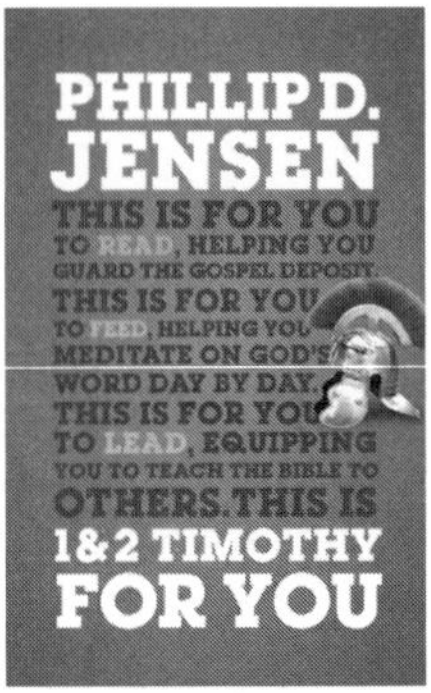

1 & 2 Timothy For You

If you are reading *1 & 2 Timothy For You* alongside this Good Book Guide, here is how the studies in this booklet link to the chapters of *1 & 2 Timothy For You:*

Study One > Ch 1-2
Study Two > Ch 3-4
Study Three > Ch 5-6
Study Four > Ch 7
Study Five > Ch 8-9
Study Six > Ch 9-10
Study Seven > Ch 11

Find out more about *1 & 2 Timothy For You* at:
www.thegoodbook.com/for-you

1 & 2 Timothy: Guard the Gospel
A Good Book Guide

This edition printed 2026.

Published by The Good Book Company

thegoodbook.com | thegoodbook.co.uk
thegoodbook.com.au | thegoodbook.co.nz

Every book published by The Good Book Company has been written by a human author and edited by a human editor. While AI tools are sometimes used to assist with research and support certain processes, all content has been created by a human author and thoroughly checked by our editorial team to ensure it is biblically faithful and pastorally wise.

A CIP catalogue record for this book is available from the British Library.

Design by André Parker and Drew McCall

ISBN: 9781802541960 | JOB-008712 | Printed in India

Contents

Introduction

One of the Bible writers described God's word as "a lamp for my feet, a light on my path" (Psalm 119:105, NIV). God gave us the Bible to tell us about who he is and what he wants for us. He speaks through it by his Spirit and lights our way through life.

That means that we need to look carefully at the Bible and uncover its meaning—but we also need to apply what we've discovered to our lives.

Good Book Guides are designed to help you do just that. The sessions in this book are interactive and easy to lead. They're perfect for use in groups or for personal study.

Let's take a look at what is included in each session.

Talkabout: Every session starts with an ice-breaker question, designed to get people talking around a subject that links to the Bible study.

Investigate: These questions help you explore what the passage is about.

Apply: These questions are designed to get you thinking practically: what does this Bible teaching mean for you and your church?

Explore More: These optional sections help you to go deeper or to explore another part of the Bible which connects with the main passage.

Getting Personal: These sections are a chance for personal reflection. Some groups may feel comfortable discussing these, but you may prefer to look at them quietly as individuals instead—or leave them out.

Pray: Here, you're invited to pray in the light of the truths and challenges you've seen in the study.

Each session is also designed to be easily split into two! Watch out for the **Apply** section that comes halfway through, and stop there if you haven't got time to do the whole thing in one go.

In the back of the book, you'll find a **Leader's Guide**, which provides helpful notes on every question, along with everything else that group leaders need in order to facilitate a great session and help the group uncover the riches of God's light-giving word.

Why Study 1 & 2 Timothy?

The two letters Paul wrote to his protégé Timothy were inspired by God for our learning. As Paul talks to his closest colleague, these letters give us a deep insight into the thinking of the great missionary apostle to the nations.

Nowhere can we get closer to Paul's mind than when he's talking to his true child in the faith, Timothy. While the two men were often separated, as they were when Paul wrote these letters, they also travelled together and spent time with each other (2 Corinthians 1:1; Colossians 1:1). And their closeness is nowhere more evident than in 2 Timothy, when Paul is coming to the end of his missionary endeavours and wishes to pass the baton on to his "son".

Yet these letters were not for Timothy alone—they reveal God's plan for our lives as well. Paul wrote 1 Timothy with a consciousness of a wider audience than that one man; and even the more private 2 Timothy contains the apostle's teaching, to be handed down to others who will in turn teach still others (2 Timothy 2:2).

The context of 1 and 2 Timothy is the Christian mission. Christianity is missionary at heart. Jesus himself was on a mission: he was sent by his Father and "came into the world to save sinners" (1 Timothy 1:15).

All Christians are missionaries. A missionary is not somebody who travels overseas. The essence is not the travel but the purpose-directed life of taking the gospel to others. To be a disciple of Jesus is to be a missionary.

1 and 2 Timothy are classic examples of missionary letters. In 1 Timothy Paul tells Timothy how to conduct himself in Paul's temporary absence (1 Timothy 3:14-15). In 2 Timothy Paul tells Timothy how to succeed him in the mission after he has gone (2 Timothy 4:1-8).

Because all Christians are engaged in the mission of Christ, the letters of the great missionary apostle, Paul, are obviously important to us. In particular, his advice and instructions to his closest colleague are invaluable in framing our own lives as missionaries, as we seek, like Timothy, to guard the gospel.

1 & 2 Timothy 49–68 AD

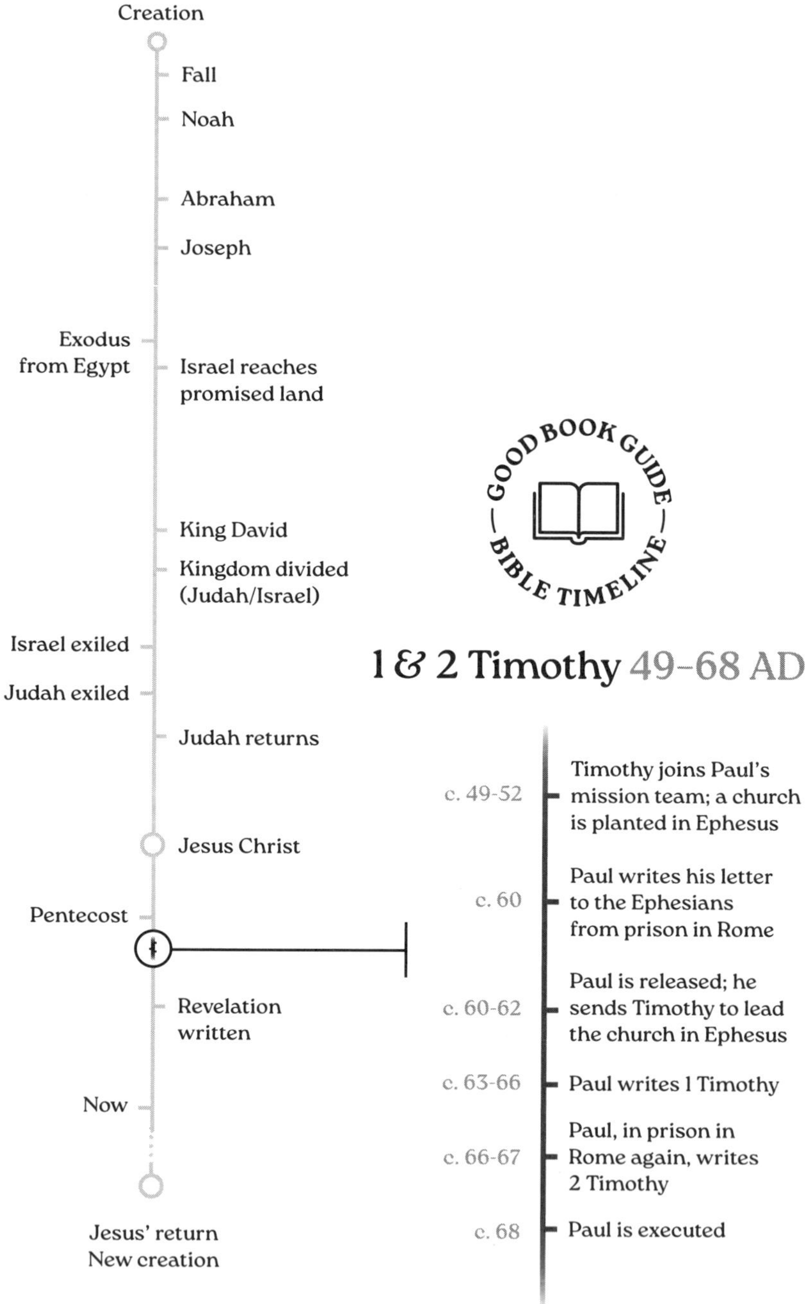

1

Christ Came to Save

1 Timothy 1:1-17

Talkabout

1. Imagine writing to a younger Christian living in a different country. Think of three things you might want to tell them.

Investigate

Read 1 Timothy 1:1-7

DICTIONARY

Apostle (v 1): "apostle" means "sent". The apostles were sent by Jesus to continue his mission to save sinners.

Doctrine (v 3): teaching.
Genealogy (v 4): line of descent from an ancestor.

2. How does Paul describe himself (v 1) and Timothy (v 2)?

- What does this tell you about these two men?

3. What does Paul want Timothy to do (v 3-4)?

- How does this compare with the reason why Paul writes his letter? (See 1 Timothy 3:14-15.)

Apply

4. Increasingly today, any opinion that may divide or even cause any offence in society is silenced. But Paul says the aim of his charge to Timothy is *love* (v 5). So how can we lovingly challenge false teaching when we come across it?

5. Paul warns Timothy about "vain discussion", when people are without any real understanding of what's being said (v 7). It's good to ask questions as we discuss the Bible with others, but how can we avoid that becoming pointless discussion?

Getting Personal | OPTIONAL

When are you particularly tempted to get involved with vain discussions (either directly with others or online)?

How can you avoid getting into such situations?

Investigate

📖 **Read 1 Timothy 1:8-17**

DICTIONARY

Blasphemer (v 13): someone who speaks in an evil way about God.

6. Paul says that the law is good (v 8). Who is the law not for (v 9)?

7. Verses 9-10 list the reasons why a lawless world needs the law. This list largely follows the pattern of the Ten Commandments, but it uses strong and extreme examples for each of them. Fill in the gaps in this table:

The Ten Commandments (from Exodus 20)	Examples of lawless behaviour from 1 Timothy 1:9-17
No other gods (v 3)	
No idols (v 4-6)	Sinners (v 9)
No blasphemy (v 7)	
Keep the rest day holy (v 8-11)	

The Ten Commandments (from Exodus 20)	**Examples of lawless behaviour from 1 Timothy 1:9-17**
Honour parents (v 12)	
No killing (v 13)	
No adultery (v 14)	The sexually immoral (v 10)
No stealing (v 15)	
No false witness (v 16)	
No coveting (v 17)	(Not included in ch. 1, but Paul does address greed in 1 Timothy 6:9-10.)

Explore More | OPTIONAL

Paul says that the law is good (v 8).

- How would you answer the following two wrong views of the law?
  - We don't need the law because we have the Spirit. (See Galatians 5:16.)
  - We don't need the law because we are justified by grace. (See Galatians 5:13-14.)

8. How does Paul describe himself in verses 13 and 15?

- Why was such a view crucial for him then, and why is it crucial for us now, in order to receive the gospel (v 15)?

9. Twice in verses 12-16, Paul says that he "received mercy". What reason does he give each time?
   - v 13

   - v 16

   - Is this what you expected? Why / why not?

10. When Paul was still known as Saul of Tarsus (Acts 9:1-2), he didn't believe in Jesus, and he hated those who followed him. How did Jesus change Saul (v 14)?

Getting Personal | OPTIONAL

Paul received mercy because of Christ's "perfect patience" (v 16). Looking back at your own life, how was Jesus patient with you before you came to faith? Or, if you can't remember a time when you didn't love and follow Jesus, how has he patiently enabled you to grow in your love for him?

Think of someone who doesn't yet know Jesus. Pray that Jesus will patiently bring them to himself. Pray that you will play your part in sharing his gospel with them.

Apply

11. List two people you want to share the gospel with. In each case, do you think they need to receive mercy because of ignorance (they genuinely believe that their views on Jesus are correct) or defiance (having heard the gospel, they choose to turn their backs on God)?

12. For each person named in question 11, write down one thing you will do this week to help them move on in their understanding or to challenge them in their defiance.

Pray

"To the King of ages, immortal, invisible, the only God, be honour and glory for ever and ever. Amen." (1 Timothy 1:17)

Take each section of verse 17 in turn and use it to praise and thank God.

2

Men and Women of the Gospel

1 Timothy 1:18 – 3:13

The Story So Far...

Paul charges Timothy (and us) to guard the gospel and to challenge those who teach anything different. Through this gospel we have received mercy.

Talkabout

1. How do you tend to react when the Bible says something that disagrees with modern culture?

Investigate

📖 **Read 1 Timothy 1:18 – 2:7**

DICTIONARY

Supplications, intercessions (2:1): asking or requesting.

Mediator (v 5): one who brings about reconciliation.
Gentiles (v 7): non-Jews.

Timothy has been charged to silence false teachers (1:3) and hold faith (1:19). These next verses show all of us how "to behave in the household of God" (3:15).

2. Who are we urged to pray for in 2:1-2, and why is this good (v 2-3)?

3. What do we learn about God, and about Jesus the Son of God, in verses 4-6?

Pray

Now would be a great moment to pray!

Use verse 2 to shape how you pray for leaders in your country. Then thank and praise God for the things you've learned about him in verses 4-6. Finally, ask God to help you as you read and discuss the rest of today's passage. Ask him to help you to trust that his words in the Bible are good and to discuss them in a way that is helpful to others in your group.

Investigate

Read 1 Timothy 2:8-15

DICTIONARY

Transgressor (v 14): law-breaker.

4. These verses show us part of what godly living looks like for both men and women. What do we learn about men?

   - What do we learn about women?

5. What do you find most attractive about these verses? What do you find most challenging?

Getting Personal | OPTIONAL

You may find some of what is said in these verses hard to accept. If not, you'll almost certainly know someone who does.

Ask God to help you think about such things biblically. Ask him to help you to trust that his words in the Bible are always good.

Apply

6. *If you are a man:* How is your prayer life? What can you do to remind yourself to pray and broaden the range of those you pray for?
   If you are a woman: How can you "adorn yourself" in a way that is consistent with your Christian faith?

7. Paul addresses the manner in which we behave—the manner in which men pray (v 8) and the manner in which women learn (v 11). Why do you think this matters?

Investigate

Read 1 Timothy 3:1-13

DICTIONARY

Deacon (v 8): servant.

Titles such as priest, deacon, bishop and elder come from this passage, but are used differently from one church to another. So we need to be careful to read what Paul does say, without tying it too closely to our own particular use of those terms. These verses address the work of overseers (v 1-7) and deacons/servants (v 8-13).

8. Christian leadership is very different from the world's leadership. What does Paul say are the characteristics of a Christian leader?

- How do these compare to the characteristics of some of the leaders we read about in the media?

Explore More | OPTIONAL

Both overseers and deacons are to avoid getting drunk (v 3, 8).

Read Proverbs 31:4-5

- How was a leader's relationship with alcohol spelled out by King Lemuel's mother?

---

9. An overseer "must not be a recent convert" (v 6) and "must be well thought of by outsiders" (v 7). What reasons does Paul give for this?

- Can you think of any other reasons why these two characteristics matter?

Apply

10. Christian leadership is "a noble task" (v 1) but also a hard one. What could you do a) this week and b) this month to help the pastor of your church or the leader of your group to be a faithful leader?

11. Both lists address the dangers of abusing speech, alcohol and money. Which of these is most likely to be a temptation for you, whether you are a leader or not? How will you handle that temptation this week?

Getting Personal | OPTIONAL

We are never more like Jesus than when we serve others well (Mark 10:42-45; Philippians 2:5-11).

Whatever your role in your church, how will you serve your fellow Christians well this week?

Pray

Look back at your answers to questions 10 and 11. Pray for the Lord's help in doing the things you have listed there.

3

Godliness Training

1 Timothy 3:14 - 6:2

The Story So Far...

Paul charges Timothy (and us) to guard the gospel and to challenge those who teach anything different. Through this gospel we have received mercy.

Paul shows us what godly living looks like for both men and women, leaders and servants in the household of God (the local church).

Talkabout

1. Choose three words to describe Jesus. Why did you pick those three?

Investigate

1 Timothy 3:14 – 4:16

DICTIONARY

Manifested (3:16): appeared; revealed.
Holy (4:5): set apart; pure.

Exhortation (4:13): urging; strong encouragement.

The essence of godliness is not our *behaviour* but our *relationship* with God. A modern guide to godliness might be a list of things to do and not to do, but what Paul gives Timothy is a list of things that God has already done in Christ Jesus.

2. In question 1, you thought of three words to describe Jesus. In 3:16, what six things does Paul tell us about Jesus, and what do you think each one means?
   -
   -
   -
   -
   -
   -

3. What reason does Paul give for some "departing from the faith" (4:1), and how do they hear these wrong teachings (4:2)?

4. Verse 3 gives an example of false teaching. What was being taught, and how does Paul counter that in verses 3-5?

Explore More | OPTIONAL

Timothy isn't the only person Paul warned about the dangers of rule-based moralism.

Read Colossians 2:20-23

- What rules had the Colossian Christians made for themselves?
- Can you think of modern-day equivalents?

Pray that the Lord will help you and your church to avoid this kind of religious rule-making.

5. Which words in 4:13, 15 and 16 show how committed Timothy needs to be to the ministry of the word of God? What will be the result (v 15, 16)?

Apply

Like Timothy, we cannot stop someone thinking negatively about us, but we can remove any reason for the negativity. We can even provide, in speech and conduct, some reason for them to think positively about us (v 12).

6. How might this apply to your life this week:
   - in your church relationships?

   - with those outside of church?

Getting Personal | OPTIONAL

Is there someone in your life who has good reason for thinking negatively about you? Ask God to forgive you. How will you put this right?

Investigate

📖 **1 Timothy 5:1 – 6:2**

DICTIONARY

The adversary (5:14): the enemy, Satan.

Elect angels (5:21): angels who will be with Jesus when he returns as our Judge (Mark 8:38).

7. When Paul wrote this letter, Timothy was a young man. How was he to treat those in the church family: older men, younger men, older women and younger women?

8. The question of honouring widows takes the next 14 verses (v 3-16). What are the four kinds of widows Paul refers to, and who should take care of them?
   - v 4
   - v 5
   - v 6

- v 11

Getting Personal | OPTIONAL

How are widows looked after in your church? How can you help care for them (as an individual or as part of a group)?

As well as honouring widows, we are to honour elders (5:17-19), and slaves are to honour their masters (6:1-2).

9. How are elders to be honoured (5:18-19)?

    - How and why should slaves honour their masters (6:1-2)?

10. 1 Timothy 5:19 outlines how to protect elders from false accusations. How was Timothy to deal with true accusations (v 20)?

Apply

11. In 1 Timothy 5:1 – 6:2, Paul shows us that we honour God by honouring others. How will the motivation of bringing glory to God make a difference to how you honour others this week?

Pray

📖 Reread 1 Timothy 3:16

Divide the six statements among you (repeating some if your group has more than six people). Take it in turns to use your statement(s) to thank and praise Christ.

4

The Great Gain of Godliness

1 Timothy 6:2-21

The Story So Far...

Paul charges Timothy (and us) to guard the gospel and to challenge those who teach anything different. Through this gospel we have received mercy.

Paul shows us what godly living looks like for both men and women, leaders and servants in the household of God (the local church).

The essence of godliness is not our behaviour but our relationship with God. We honour God by honouring others.

Talkabout

1. Who is the most contented person you know? What do you think is the secret of their contentment?

Investigate

Read 1 Timothy 6:2-10

DICTIONARY

Doctrine (v 3): teaching.

2. What happens to the person who "teaches a different doctrine" (v 3-4)?

   • What is the result of this false teaching (v 4-5)?

3. In verse 5, those who listen to false teaching are described as "imagining that godliness is a means of gain". But in verse 6, Paul states that "there is great gain in godliness". How can both of these be true?

4. A desire to be richer (whether in money, possessions or experiences) breeds discontent. What strong words and phrases does Paul use to show what happens when we approach life in this way (v 9-10)?

   • What terrible result has Paul seen in the lives of some people in the church (v 10)?

Explore More | OPTIONAL

Read 2 Corinthians 8:1-9

- How was the church in Macedonia in many ways the opposite of what Paul warns against in 1 Timothy 6:9-10?
- What is the key to this kind of generous contentment, does 2 Corinthians 8:9 suggest?

Apply

5. Do you find it easy to agree with Paul that "if we have food and clothing, with these we will be content"? Why / why not?

- Do you find it easier to be content when you have much or when you have little? (See Paul's view of contentment in Philippians 4:10-13.)

Getting Personal | OPTIONAL

Do you sometimes struggle with contentment? If so, are there ungodly responses you need to repent of? (For example, do you complain when someone else has something you want, or do you spend a lot of time and energy chasing after things you think will make you happy?)

6. How does living a godly life model contentment to those around you? What impact do you think this will have on other Christians and on those who are not Christians?

Investigate

📖 **Read 1 Timothy 6:11-21**

DICTIONARY

Righteousness (v 11): to be right with God.

Pontius Pilate (v 13): Roman governor of Judea when Jesus was crucified.

Dominion (v 16): rule as king.

7. What is Timothy told to pursue in verse 11?

Getting Personal | OPTIONAL

Quietly read through verses 15-16 to yourself. How does this description of our awesome God make you feel? It is only because of Jesus that we can approach this God who "dwells in unapproachable light". Thank him for this now.

8. Back in verses 9-10, we were warned about the danger of riches. What kind of riches are we encouraged to pursue instead in verses 17-19?

Apply

9. Would someone who knows you describe you as rich in wealth, or in good works and generosity (or neither)?

- What can you change this week to be the second kind of rich man or woman?

- How has this passage motivated you to be that person?

10. In verses 11-12 Timothy is told to *pursue*, to *fight* and to *take hold*. These are all very active terms. Do you think you are this active in living for Christ? Is there something more you could be doing?

Pray

Paul starts and ends this letter by praying for grace for Timothy (1:2 and 6:21). Pray now for each member of your group to know God's grace and to be able, through his grace and the working of the Spirit, to live godly lives that bring honour to our Lord.

5

Do Not Be Ashamed

2 Timothy 1:1 - 2:13

Talkabout

1. When you're with non-Christian friends or family, how do you feel about sharing the gospel?

- How would you define "Christian ministry"? Who does it, and what does it involve?

Investigate

Read 2 Timothy 1:1-18

DICTIONARY

Manifested (v 10): revealed.
That Day (v 12, 18): when Jesus returns as our Judge.
Rendered (v 18): gave, provided.

2. What do these verses tell us about…
    - Paul?
    - Timothy?
    - the relationship between them?

3. What does Paul tell Timothy to do in verse 6?
    - What does verse 7 show us this will look like?

4. What does Paul tell Timothy to do (and not to do) in verse 8?
    - How would verses 9-14 encourage Timothy to obey Paul's commands in verse 8?

Explore More | OPTIONAL

Read 2 Corinthians 11:23-29; Philippians 1:12-18; Romans 1:14-17

- What do these passages tell us about what Paul experienced in the course of his ministry?
- What do they tell us about what Paul prioritised during his ministry?

5. What positive examples of obeying verse 8, and contrasting examples of disobeying, do we see in verses 15-18?

Apply

6. In what contexts is it most tempting to be "ashamed" of the gospel, or of other Christians?

7. What would it look like to follow Paul's "pattern" (v 13) in those situations? How would the truths of verses 9-12 motivate and empower us?

Getting Personal | OPTIONAL

"I am not ashamed of the gospel, for it is the power of God for salvation to everyone who believes." (Romans 1:16)

What will it mean for you to be confident in the gospel's power, rather than ashamed of its message, this week?

Investigate

Read 2 Timothy 2:1-13

DICTIONARY

Offspring of David (v 8): from King David's family line.

The elect (v 10): chosen by God.

Remember, Paul is in prison. Later in the letter he says that he expects that "the time of my departure has come ... I have finished the race" (4:6-7).

8. Why does that make the command of 2:2 crucial for the church?

9. To what three jobs does Paul compare the task of gospel teaching and gospel sharing (v 3-6)?

- What does Paul want to show us about Christian ministry?

10. How would Paul, "bound with chains as a criminal" (v 9), and Timothy, facing the struggles of Christian ministry, be encouraged by the truths of...
    - verse 8?

    - verses 11b-13?

    - How would those truths motivate them to "endure everything for the sake of the elect" (v 10)?

Apply

11. Having read Paul's message to Timothy from 1:1 – 2:13, what words would you use to describe Christian ministry?

12. What happens to our own ministry if we forget...
    - that ministry involves suffering?

    - that ministry requires self-discipline?

- that Christ has risen, is guarding us, and will bring his people to life with him?

- that the Spirit gives us power, love and self-control?

Getting Personal | OPTIONAL

How does this study need to reshape your expectations about and commitment to the ministry God has called you to?

Pray

"Do not be ashamed of the testimony about our Lord … but share in suffering for the gospel." (2 Timothy 1:8)

Confess ways in which you have been ashamed, or have sought to avoid suffering for the gospel.

"Our Saviour Christ Jesus … abolished death and brought life and immortality to light through the gospel." (2 Timothy 1:10)

Praise God for all that he accomplished through the life, death and resurrection of his Son, Jesus.

"God gave us a spirit not of fear but of power and love and self-control." (2 Timothy 1:7)

Ask God's Spirit to grow these things in your spirit, so that you will be ready to speak boldly of the gospel to those around you. Share with one another specific ways in which you need the Spirit to give you power, love and self-control.

Finish by saying together the words of 2 Timothy 2:11-13.

6

Work and Life in the Last Days

2 Timothy 2:14 - 3:17

The Story So Far...

Paul told Timothy not to be ashamed of the gospel—because, despite the opposition to it, the gospel is powerful, Christ has risen, and eternity is secured.

Talkabout

1. If you had to sum up your expectations for your Christian life in a ten-word sentence, what would you say?

Investigate

📖 **Read 2 Timothy 2:14-26**

DICTIONARY

The word of truth (v 15): Scripture, the Bible.

Iniquity (v 19): wickedness.

2. In what ways are Timothy and the "faithful men" he works with (the "them" of verse 14) to use their words (v 14-15, 23-25)?

3. What does Paul warn them about (v 16-18)?

- Why (v 14b, 16, 18)?

- How do verses 20-22 motivate Timothy in this kind of life and work?

4. In verses 22-26, what is the link between the way Timothy is to live and the words he is to say, do you think?

Getting Personal | OPTIONAL

It is so important that we not only teach the truth but also teach it truthfully—that we exemplify the message that we are teaching.

How does that encourage you, and/or challenge you—in what you say (and don't say), and in how you act (and don't act)?

Apply

5. In what situations—with Christians as well as in the wider world—do you find it easy to misuse your words?

- How could you "rightly handle the word of truth" in those contexts?

Investigate

📖 **Read 2 Timothy 3:1-17**

DICTIONARY

Sacred writings, Scripture (v 15, 16): the Bible.

Reproof (v 16): rebuke, reprimand.

6. What should Timothy expect as he seeks to live as a Christian?
   - v 1
   - v 2-4
   - v 6-7

Verse 5 is the key text of verses 1-9. People will be "having the appearance of godliness, but denying its power". Such people do not believe what the gospel teaches but are involved in what the Christian community does.

7. What should Timothy do in response to these people (v 5)?

- What do you think this means in practice?

Explore More | OPTIONAL

Jannes and Jambres were, in Jewish tradition, the names of the magicians in Pharaoh's court who opposed Moses and Aaron when they asked Pharaoh to let God's people leave Egypt.

Scan-read Exodus 7:8 – 8:19

- What were Jannes and Jambres able to do when Aaron's staff turned into a serpent… the Nile turned to blood… and frogs infested the country (7:11-12, 22; 8:7)?
- What were they able to do when the dust became gnats (8:18)?
- What did they therefore realise (v 19)?
- How does this show the truth of Paul's claim in 2 Timothy 3:9?
- How have you seen this to be the case in your own life as a Christian?

Paul has shown Timothy what life will be like as a Christian between Jesus' ascension and return ("the last days", v 1).

8. How should he respond?
    - v 10-11: By following…
    - v 12-13: By remembering…
    - v 14-17: By continuing…

9. Why should the Bible be at the centre of every Christian's life (v 15-17)?

Apply

10. How can you follow Paul's instructions in verses 10-17, and help one another to do this?

11. If you now had to sum up your expectations for your Christian life in a ten-word sentence, what would you say?

Pray

Spend time praising God for his word. You can use what Paul reminds us about the Scriptures in verses 15-17 to fuel your thanksgiving.

Then use your answers to question 8 to ask God to help you, individually and as a church, to accept hardship and even persecution as you seek to correctly handle the word of truth in the last days. Share with one another specific areas where doing this is costly for you personally.

7

I Charge You...

2 Timothy 4:1-22

The Story So Far...

Paul told Timothy not to be ashamed of the gospel—because, despite the opposition to it, the gospel is powerful, Christ has risen and eternity is secured.

Paul has explained that normal Christian living involves suffering, but we are to serve our Master by living out his word, and by using our words to proclaim his.

Talkabout

1. What makes someone a good church leader?

Investigate

📖 Read 2 Timothy 4:1-5

DICTIONARY

Exhort (v 2): urge, encourage.

2. How does Paul underline the seriousness of the "charge" he is giving Timothy here (v 1)?

The main command of the charge is simply "preach the word" (v 2). "Preach" does not mean stand in a pulpit, but rather, "proclaim" or "declare". The word of God is not a discussion-starter but a declaration. As the prophets of old would say, "Thus says the Lord..."

Getting Personal | OPTIONAL

When the God-breathed word is preached, it is God speaking to you.

Think about how you approach sermons Sunday by Sunday. Does anything need to change in how you listen to, respond to and seek to remember what is said?

---

3. In verses 2 and 5, Paul tells Timothy how he must "preach the word". For each subordinate command, think through what this would have required of Timothy in his everyday ministry.
    - Be ready in season and out of season

    - Reprove, rebuke and exhort

    - With complete patience and teaching

- Be sober-minded

- Endure suffering

- Do the work of an evangelist

- Fulfil your ministry

4. Why will this task be difficult (v 3-4)?

Apply

5. "A faithful pastor will not often be a popular one." To what extent is this true, do you think?

6. To what extent does your church value in your pastor(s) the characteristics Paul called for in Timothy?

    - How can you show your pastor(s) your appreciation for the ways in which they fulfil this ministry?

Investigate

📖 **Read 2 Timothy 4:6-8**

DICTIONARY

Drink offering (v 6): in Old Testament Israel, an offering of wine or water was poured on top of a sacrifice presented to God.

7. How does Paul view his life, and his death?

8. How does this add gravity and urgency to his "charge" to Timothy?

Read 2 Timothy 4:9-22

9. What insights do these verses give us into:
   - Paul's friendships?

   - Paul's hardships?

   - Paul's priorities?

Apply

10. How should Paul's example here shape the way we view the whole concept of "retirement"?

11. How should Paul's example here shape our view of what matters most in life?

Explore More | OPTIONAL

Scan-read the whole of 1 and 2 Timothy

- What does Paul remind Timothy about...
  - who Jesus is and what we enjoy through faith in him?
  - what Christian ministry involves?
  - what life will be like for the committed Christian?

12. Through 1 and 2 Timothy, in what ways has the Spirit of "power and love and self-control" (2 Timothy 1:7) been encouraging and challenging you to guard the gospel deposit that has been entrusted to you (v 14)?

Getting Personal | OPTIONAL

Reflect on your answers to question 12. In what tangible ways are you being called to change? How will you make progress in those areas?

Pray

Use your answers to question 12 to shape both your prayers of praise and of petition.

1 & 2 Timothy

Guard the Gospel

LEADER'S GUIDE

Leader's Guide: Introduction

This Leader's Guide includes guidance for every question. It will provide background information and help you if you get stuck. For each session, you'll also find the following:

The Big Idea: The main point of the session, in brief. This is what you should be aiming to have fixed in people's minds by the end of the session!

Summary: An overview of the passage you're reading together.

Optional Extra: Usually this is an introductory activity that ties in with the main theme of the Bible study and is designed to break the ice at the beginning of a session. Or it may be a "homework project" that people can tackle during the week.

Occasionally the Leader's Guide includes an extra follow-up question, printed in ***italics***. This doesn't appear in the main study guide but could be a useful add-on to help your group get to the answer or go deeper.

Here are a few key principles to bear in mind as you prepare to lead:

- Don't just read out the answers from the Leader's Guide. Ideally, you want the group to discover these answers from the Bible for themselves.
- Keep drawing people back to the passage you're studying. People may come up with answers based on their experiences or on teaching they've heard in the past, but the point of this study is to listen to God's word itself—so keep directing your group to look at the text.
- Make sure everyone finishes the session knowing how the passage is relevant for them. We do Bible study so that our lives can be changed by what we hear from God's word. So, **Apply** questions aren't just an add-on—they're a vital part of the session.

Finally, remember that your group is unique! You should feel free to use this Good Book Guide in a way that works for them. If they're a quiet bunch, you might want to spend longer on the **Talkabout** question. If they love to get creative, try using mind-mapping or doodling to kick-start some of your discussions. If your time is limited, you can choose to skip **Explore More** or split the whole session into two. Adapt the material in whatever way you think will help your group get the most out of God's word.

1

Christ Came to Save

1 Timothy 1:1-17

The Big Idea

Paul charges Timothy (and us) to guard the gospel and to challenge those who teach anything different. The aim of this charge is love (v 5). Through the gospel we have "received mercy" (v 13, 16).

Summary

1 Timothy 1:1-2 starts with the sender (Paul) and then the recipient (Timothy), and then adds Paul's usual well-wishing greeting, wishing grace and peace (and, in Timothy's case, mercy, v 2) for those he's writing to (as in Galatians 1:3; 2 Thessalonians 1:2).

However, the opening greeting tells us a little more than simply that this letter was from Paul to Timothy. It emphasises that Paul is "an apostle of Christ Jesus by the command of God our Saviour and of Christ Jesus our hope" (1 Timothy 1:1). Furthermore, he describes Timothy as "my true child in the faith". Timothy was not Paul's biological son, but he was his spiritual child. Paul was Timothy's mentor, as Timothy was Paul's protégé.

This letter is not a private correspondence but intended to be a public letter of recommendation for Timothy, who is facing a difficult task of waging the good warfare and fighting the good fight (1 Timothy 1:18; 6:12). He has to charge certain people not to teach different doctrines (1:3). He is going to have to teach and give commands (4:11; 6:2, 17). He is going to have to deal with disciplining elders and commanding rich people (5:21; 6:17). He has to deal with people older than himself who could be tempted to despise him for his youth (4:12; 5:1). This letter would give him the backing of the apostle, both personally and to anybody to whom he cared to show it.

Paul had hoped to come to Timothy soon, but now he was possibly going to delay his arrival. That delay is the reason Paul gives for writing this letter (3:14-15). This is Paul's explicit reason for writing to Timothy. If we are to understand the letter, we must pay careful attention to this passage.

Paul writes to Timothy about "how one ought to behave" (3:15), especially as one who has responsibility to teach, urge and command others. It is not about how he may like to behave but about the moral imperative of how he ought to behave.

Timothy is to charge people to stop teaching "different doctrine". "Doctrine" simply means "teaching". At first glance, it doesn't appear that Timothy is told how to charge these persons to stop their teaching. He is not given the authority of government nor any power of coercion. Yet, on reflection, the whole letter is about how he is to behave in such a way that he will be able to deliver this charge. It is by the prophecies made about Timothy and the gift that God has given him by prophecy that he is to wage the good warfare, and fight the good fight (1:18; 4:14; 6:12). It is by devoting himself to "the public reading of Scripture, to exhortation, to teaching" (4:13). It is by his life and doctrine that he will save himself and his hearers (4:16). In other words, his conduct and his teaching must exemplify his stand against the false teachers.

Paul concludes this section in verse 17 with a wonderful doxology: "To the King of the ages, immortal, invisible, the only God, be honour and glory for ever and ever. Amen."

Optional Extra

Give each person a piece of card. Ask them to copy out 1 Timothy 1:15, including the Bible reference. (The act of writing something down helps us to remember it.) Spend a few minutes memorising this verse—you could come back to it at the end of the study as well. Encourage group members to keep the card tucked into their Bibles while you explore 1 Timothy together.

Guidance for Questions

1. **Imagine writing to a younger Christian living in a different country. Think of three things you might want to tell them.**
   Don't let this conversation go on for too long. The idea is to help group members put themselves in a similar situation to Paul, who was writing to encourage a younger Christian.

2. **How does Paul describe himself (v 1) and Timothy (v 2)?**
   Paul is "an apostle of Christ Jesus by command of God our Saviour and of Christ Jesus our hope" (v 1). Paul describes Timothy as his "true child in the faith" (v 2).

- **What does this tell you about these two men?**
  An apostle was somebody who was sent on a mission—something like an ambassador. Christ's apostles were sent to continue and implement his mission, which was to save sinners (1 Timothy 1:15). Paul didn't choose this role for himself (in fact, his chosen role had been to persecute the first Christians, not to join them—Acts 9:1-2). Instead, he was "commanded" to be an apostle by God himself (Acts 9:15). The close relationship between Paul and Timothy is shown by Paul calling Timothy his "child". Timothy was not Paul's biological son, but he was his spiritual child. Paul was Timothy's mentor, as Timothy was Paul's protégé.

3. **What does Paul want Timothy to do (v 3-4)?**
   He wants Timothy to stay where he is in Ephesus (in modern Turkey). Timothy is to "charge certain persons" in the church there. He is to tell them not to teach a different doctrine from the one Paul taught when he was with them. Timothy is also to tell them to avoid "myths and endless genealogies".

   Myths: Christian teaching is based

in history and eyewitness evidence. See, for example, 2 Peter 1:16: "For we did not follow cleverly devised myths when we made known to you the power and coming of our Lord Jesus Christ, but we were eyewitnesses of his majesty".

Genealogies: The Bible has a few genealogies and they do raise quite significant questions. Unlike modern genealogies, which have as their prime goal complete detailed accuracy, the Bible's genealogies have some teaching point in mind. (For example, Matthew 1 paves the way for the extraordinary birth of Christ by (unusually) mentioning some female ancestors of Jesus—Rahab the prostitute, Ruth the Moabite widow, and Bathsheba the "wife of Uriah", with whom David committed adultery.) However, genealogies, by their very nature, are open to endless detailed discussion, so we are warned both here and in Titus 3 to "avoid foolish controversies, genealogies, dissensions, and quarrels about the law, for they are unprofitable and worthless" (Titus 3:9).

- **How does this compare with the reason why Paul writes his letter? (See 1 Timothy 3:14-15.)**

Paul wrote his letter so that "you may know how you ought to behave in the household of God" (1 Timothy 3:15). Timothy has the responsibility to teach, urge and command others, and he must behave in such a way that his life backs up what he teaches. Paul confirms the link between these two aspects later in the letter when he tells Timothy to "keep a close watch on yourself and on the teaching" (1 Timothy 4:16). This is just as important for our leaders today, so we will want to pray for them that the Lord will enable them to live godly lives as well as teach us Bible truths. 1 Timothy 3:14-16 is the key to understanding the whole letter. We will come back to these verses in later studies.

4. **Increasingly today, any opinion that may divide or even cause any offence in society is silenced. But Paul says the aim of his charge to Timothy is *love* (v 5). So how can we lovingly challenge false teaching when we come across it?**

In our modern world, "tolerance" is king, so we are seen as unloving if we challenge what other people believe or teach. But it is *always* loving to teach truth about God. We will want to be careful about how we do it—the words we use, the tone of voice, the moment we choose—but the most loving thing anyone can do is point people to Jesus, the one who loves us so much that he came into the world to save us (1 Timothy 1:15).

5. **Paul warns Timothy about "vain discussion", when people are without any real understanding of what's being said (v 7). It's good to ask questions as we discuss the Bible with others, but how can**

we avoid that becoming pointless discussion?

If you are doing this study with a group, there are likely to be a mix of characters. Some will say little while others love to debate every point! It can help to keep two questions in mind: 1) Is your discussion focused on the Bible text or have you become distracted by a red herring? 2) Does your discussion lead to a change in how group members live for Christ (3:15)?

6. **Paul says that the law is good (v 8). Who is the law not for (v 9)?**

It is not for "the just". People who are just and/or righteous (the Greek word in verse 9 can mean either, or both) do not need the law to condemn them or constrain them. They do what is right.

The opposite of "the just" is shown in verses 9-10. The law is given for people who are not right—in particular the "lawless" (v 9) who live out their lawlessness in immorality. This doesn't mean the law is irrelevant for Christians. This is the law that is written on our hearts by the Spirit who moves us to obey it (Jeremiah 31:33).

7. **Verses 9-10 list the reasons why a lawless world needs the law. This list largely follows the pattern of the Ten Commandments, but it uses strong and extreme examples for each of them. Fill in the gaps in this table:**

It is easiest to fill in the lower half of the table first (starting with the treatment of parents) as this has the closest link with the Ten Commandments. Then go back to see which sinful behaviours link with the first four commandments.

Try to avoid getting caught up in long discussions about exactly what is and isn't in this list. None of the biblical lists of sinful behaviour are meant to be complete. Paul includes another one in his second letter to Timothy (2 Timothy 3:1-7), as well as more in his other letters (Romans 1:26-31; 1 Corinthians 6:9-10; Galatians 5:19-21; Ephesians 4:25-31; Colossians 3:5-8). Elsewhere, alongside warning us about sinful behaviour to avoid, Paul tells us how to respond to our fellow Christians when they do sin: "If anyone is caught in any transgression, you who are spiritual should restore him in a spirit of gentleness. Keep watch on yourself, lest you too be tempted. Bear one another's burdens, and so fulfil the law of Christ." (Galatians 6:1-2).

NOTE: If a group member questions why homosexuality is included in this list, explain that the Bible is quite clear that God forbids homosexual activity. In fact, God is opposed to all sexual activity outside of heterosexual marriage. This is a difficult topic that is best handled at another time when you are able to prepare carefully for it. *Is God Anti-Gay?* by Sam Allberry is very helpful on this subject. See page 37 for his handling of 1 Timothy 1:10.

The Ten Commandments (from Exodus 20)	Examples of lawless behaviour from 1 Timothy 1:9-17
No other gods (v 3)	The ungodly (v 9)
No idols (v 4-6)	**Sinners (v 9)**
No blasphemy (v 7)	The unholy (v 9)
Keep the rest day holy (v 8-11)	The profane (v 9)
Honour parents (v 12)	Those who strike their fathers and mothers (v 9)
No killing (v 13)	Murderers (v 9)
No adultery (v 14)	**The sexually immoral (v 10)**
No stealing (v 15)	Enslavers (this can also be translated "kidnappers"—people who steal other people) (v 10)
No false witness (v 16)	Liars and perjurers (v 10)
No coveting (v 17)	**(Not included in ch. 1, but Paul does address greed in 1 Timothy 6:9-10.)**

Explore More

- ***How would you answer the following two wrong views of the law?***
- ***We don't need the law because we have the Spirit. (See Galatians 5:16.)***

  If we are Christians, we have the Spirit living in us. He is indeed important in our struggle against our sinful nature, but that doesn't mean we don't need the law. In fact, the Spirit moves us to obey the law, not to ignore it.
- ***We don't need the law because we are justified by grace. (See Galatians 5:13-14.)***

  We are justified by God's grace—but not in order to continue in lawlessness, but to fulfil the law by our loving service of each other.

8. How does Paul describe himself in verses 13 and 15?

Paul describes himself as a blasphemer, persecutor, insolent opponent, ignorant, an unbeliever (v 13), and the foremost of sinners (v 15).

- **Why was such a view crucial for him then, and why is it crucial for us now, in order to receive the gospel (v 15)?**
  Verse 15 explains the heart of Jesus' mission: Christ "came into the world to save sinners". His mission wasn't to bring social justice or exercise miraculous powers but to save sinners. It is only when we come to Christ humbly, admitting our guilt before him, that we understand our need for the gospel.

9. **Twice in verses 12-16, Paul says that he "received mercy". What reason does he give each time?**

- **v 13**
  Paul received mercy because he "had acted ignorantly in unbelief".

- **v 16**
  Paul received mercy because of Christ's "perfect patience".

- **Is this what you expected? Why / why not?**
  Verse 13 may be a surprise. Paul had been a law-keeping Jew. He had, in his ignorance, been faithfully and sincerely following his religious convictions. This faithfulness does not in any way excuse his sinfulness. Sincerity is good, but it is insufficient to save sinners. Paul blasphemed the very God he sought to serve. He needed to receive mercy from Christ, the one with perfect patience.

10. **When Paul was still known as Saul of Tarsus (Acts 9:1-2), he didn't believe in Jesus, and he hated those who followed him. How did Jesus change Saul (v 14)?**
    The grace of Jesus overflowed for Saul/Paul. Jesus replaced his unbelief with faith, and changed his hatred to love.

11. **List two people you want to share the gospel with. In each case, do you think they need to receive mercy because of ignorance (they genuinely believe that their views on Jesus are correct) or defiance (having heard the gospel, they choose to turn their backs on God)?**
    Encourage group members to write down two names. These may be people they already talk to about Jesus, or someone new they want to share their faith with. If it's appropriate for your group, and won't break any needed confidentiality, ask group members to share the names they've chosen and whether they think these people need mercy because of ignorance or defiance.

12. **For each person named in question 11, write down one thing you will do this week to help them move on in their understanding or to challenge them in their defiance.**
    For many of us, we are more likely to take action if we have thought about it first and then committed to doing it. So encourage group members to write down what they plan to do. You may want to start the next session by asking how people have got on.

2

Men and Women of the Gospel

1 Timothy 1:18 - 3:13

The Big Idea

Paul shows us what godly living looks like, for both men and women, and leaders and servants, and he continues to unpack how "to behave in the household of God" (3:15).

Summary

As Paul has been entrusted with the gospel, so he is entrusting Timothy, his child in the faith, with the charge to silence the false teachers. But how is Timothy to fulfil his charge? The instruction given by Paul to his protégé is to pursue a gospel-based ministry. He tells Timothy how, by the mystery of godliness, to behave in the household of God (3:15-16).

Paul tells Timothy to start with "prayers" (2:1). The apostle's command to pray is not about prayer regarding false teachers—it's about prayer to advance the cause of the gospel mission, "for all people". He specifies certain, possibly unlikely, people to be prayed for ("kings and all who are in high positions", v 2); but the aim of such prayer is a life that will be pleasing to God our Saviour (v 3).

Following on from this, 1 Timothy 2:8-15 speaks into a controversy that has divided society and Christian thinking for the last generation. A passage such as this one that is explicitly about men (as males) and women (as females) is bound to attract attention. How does this passage fit into the cultural shift that has been happening in Western society? Is it part of the old order that needs to be swept away, or part of the new that needs to be embraced, or is it something that will need reinterpreting to be accommodated to the present reality?

Those who live under the authority of the word of God are little interested in the idea of reinterpreting the Scriptures to accommodate them to present reality. If we followed that procedure, we could safely give up the Scriptures and follow the ways of the world. So how do we, who live under God's word, approach this passage? Quite simply, we have to become indifferent to its message until we've read it carefully. Then, and only then, do we turn to reconstruct our lives and culture in the light of what it teaches. This should make us wary of our own bias—be it conservative, radical or accommodationist. We need to be resolute in working against our own bias and determining what the apostle wrote without worrying about the consequences. Only then are we in a position to turn to working out the consequences for ourselves in embracing, modifying or resisting society's changes.

This is how we need to approach not just the verses about men and women (1 Timothy 2:8-15) but also the following verses about overseers and deacons (1 Timothy 3:1-13). Whatever the minutiae of these verses, they clearly show the need for godly character, whatever our gender or our role within the household of God. This is crucially important to the health of the church, for the church is a "pillar and buttress of truth" (3:15).

NOTE: This study doesn't include a question about 1:20, but someone may ask what "handing them over to Satan" means. The exact mechanism by which somebody is handed over to Satan is not spelt out in the New Testament. In the only other reference to this phrase (1 Corinthians 5), it is something in which the entire congregation are involved. Paul's aim in handing these men over to Satan is that they may learn, or be disciplined, not to blaspheme. Paul himself was a blasphemer, though he acted in ignorance and unbelief, but they are apparently becoming blasphemers in knowledge and defiance. They are in greater danger of going beyond forgiveness (Mark 3:28-30).

Optional Extra

How many different words can you think of for praying? (Answers may include talking, requesting, intercessions, supplications, thanksgiving, praise, pleading, devotions, petitions...) Some of these will come up when Paul talks about prayer at the start of chapter 2.

Guidance for Questions

1. **How do you tend to react when the Bible says something that disagrees with modern culture?**
   This study will include some of the most hotly debated verses in 1 Timothy. The aim of the opening question is to help group members recognise whether or not they tend to struggle to accept what the Bible says if it contradicts their own beliefs or those held by modern culture. If some people admit that they will find this hard, you could pray about that when you pray together after question 3.

2. **Who are we urged to pray for in 2:1-2, and why is this good (v 2-3)?**
   - We are to pray for "all people" (v 1); then specifically for "kings and all who are in high positions" (v 2).
   - This is good because it pleases God (v 3). Also, praying for kings and leaders leads to a peaceful life (v 2). Notice it is not just governments Paul has in view here—it includes praying for any whose authority influences the lives of others. For us, it can include company CEOs, employers, judges, school principals, university professors, etc. The capacity for corruption is endless, and so the need of such people for our prayer is permanent.

3. **What do we learn about God, and about Jesus the Son of God, in verses 4-6?**
   - *About God:* There is only "one

God" (v 5), and it is his desire for "all people to be saved" (v 4). The nature of salvation is "to come to the knowledge of the truth" of the gospel (v 4). (Knowing the truth is critical to salvation. The gospel is preached and believed.)

- *About Jesus:* Jesus the Son is fully man ("the man Christ Jesus", v 5). He is the one and only "mediator between God and men" (v 5), who "gave himself as a ransom for all" (v 6).
- NOTE: A mediator is one who brings about reconciliation between two parties who are otherwise in disagreement or at war. That mediator will normally have to enjoy the confidence of both parties to persuade them to settle their accounts and make peace. Humans may want any number of mediators, but the only one acceptable to God is his Son. He became human ("the man Christ Jesus") in order to be able to represent God to us and us to God. The method of Christ's mediatory work is spelled out in verse 6—he gave himself as a ransom (Mark 10:45).
- NOTE: Verse 6b, "which is the *testimony* given at the proper time" means that Christ's ransoming is the testimony or witness to God's desire for all to be saved.

4. These verses show us part of what godly living looks like for both men and women. What do we learn about men?

Men are to pray. They are to do so "in every place" and "without anger or quarrelling" (v 8).

- **What do we learn about women?** Women are to "adorn themselves in respectable apparel, with modesty and self-control" (v 9) and "with good works" (v 10). They are to "learn quietly" (v 11) and not to "teach or to exercise authority over a man" (v 12).

5. What do you find most attractive about these verses? What do you find most challenging?

Answers will vary. The aim of this question is to help group members see the good in these verses, even if they are struggling to accept the restrictions on what women can do. Men and women who shape their lives according to these verses will point people to the Lord rather than to themselves. This will be attractive to other Christians and also to non-believers. (See *1 & 2 Timothy For You* by Phillip Jensen, pages 59-68, for a detailed unpacking of these verses. For further reading, see chapter 10 of *Women and God* by Kathleen Nielson.)

It is easy to think that men get off lightly in these verses—instead of receiving a list of things they cannot do, men are simply told to pray. But that view belittles what a life of prayer is really like. Wherever Christian men are or gather, they should pray. The essential posture is the contrite and humble heart, "lifting holy hands without anger or quarrelling" (v 8). When men pray, they must not fight.

Fighting is the opposite of prayer. And in this regard, Christian men must be holy—that is, acceptable to God. (See James 4:1-10, where the opposite of humbly praying is quarrelling and fighting.) The unholy hands that men raise are fists—and there is no place for fists in prayer. Instead, men are called to the unnatural and difficult task of praying in harmony with brothers. A man who does this will bring honour to the Lord.

NOTE: It is worth noting that this teaching in 1 Timothy 2 matches that in the rest of the New Testament, especially that of Paul, whose teaching in all the different churches is the same (1 Corinthians 4:17; 7:17; 14:33):

- *Submissiveness* is a spiritual good that is taught to all Christians (Ephesians 5:21; 1 Corinthians 16:16). It is based in our understanding of God sovereignly instituting human authority (Romans 13:1). It was demonstrated by none other than God the Son towards his human parents (Luke 2:51).
- *Teaching* is more than downloading information; it is a relational activity of leadership. So, leaders must be able to teach (1 Timothy 3:2; 4:11-12; Titus 1:9) because teachers have an authority which requires disciples (students) to follow, respect, submit to and imitate them (1 Thessalonians 5:12-13; Hebrews 13:7, 17). In this way the church is governed by the word of God rather than by power, politics, personalities or prescriptions.
- While *males and females* are created together in the image of God (Genesis 1:27), and enjoy the same status in Christ as heirs of eternal life (Galatians 3:28; 1 Peter 3:7), they continue in sexual polarity and differing responsibilities in this lifetime (1 Timothy 5; Titus 2).
- Elsewhere Paul speaks of *a rule in all the churches* about women not speaking and being in submission in the churches (1 Corinthians 14:33-35).

6. ***If you are a man:* How is your prayer life? What can you do to remind yourself to pray and broaden the range of those you pray for? *If you are a woman:* How can you "adorn yourself" in a way that is consistent with your Christian faith?**
   - *For men:* Notice that verse 8 says that men are to pray "in every place". How can you remind yourself to pray at any time in any place? Verse 1 is a reminder that we should pray for all people and for the kind of good governance that enables the gospel to go forward to all people. (For some, technology can be a great help in reminding us to pray. The PrayerMate app, which is free for both Android and iOS, is a great place to start.)
   - *For women:* Paul raises two issues concerning women: apparel and learning. The choice of adornment for the Christian woman is not the outward show of worldliness but the display of her profession of God by good works. Note that it's

not a command for *men* to adorn women in any particular fashion: just the reverse—it is a direction for women to adorn "themselves" by their wisdom and godliness. In order to make the point clearer, Paul gives four ways that would *not* be respectable or modest: braided hair, gold, pearls and costly attire. Paul is not saying that women must never under any circumstance braid their hair or wear a gold ring or pearl necklace. He is not of that legalistic mindset that details how long a skirt must fall, how high a bodice must come, or how much arm may be revealed. In fact, it is just the opposite: he is calling upon women to think for themselves about how they adorn themselves so that they can present themselves in a way that is consistent with their Christian profession.

7. **Paul addresses the manner in which we behave—the manner in which men pray (v 8) and the manner in which women learn (v 11). Why do you think this matters?**

The manner in which we do something reflects what's in our hearts. A godly life isn't about giving the appearance of obeying God. Rather, we will want to honour him in all we do and to ensure that the glory goes to him and not to us.

So, the manner in which men are to pray is by "lifting holy hands without anger or quarrelling" (v 8). The key is not the physical posture of hand-lifting. The essential posture is a contrite and humble heart. The upturned hands of a beggar are a great *symbol* of prayer—but it's not essential for Christian prayer and it's not the point of this command. Rather, the point of the hands is that they are to be "holy" and "without anger or quarrelling". When men pray, they must not fight. This is very much the point of James 4:1-10, where the opposite of humble praying is quarrelling and fighting. The unholy hands that men raise are fists—and there is no place for fists in prayer.

Likewise, a Christian woman is to undertake her learning in a Christian fashion: quietly. The word "quiet" can refer to silence, but equally it can refer to "quiet demeanour" (see 1 Peter 3:4, "the imperishable beauty of a gentle and quiet spirit"). To learn quietly is to learn with all submissiveness—that is, for a woman to place herself under authority. A woman's learning is not part of a rebellion, with the end goal of becoming the teacher and leader, but rather part of a growth in understanding in order to know how to behave as a woman who professes godliness.

8. **Christian leadership is very different from the world's leadership. What does Paul say are the characteristics of a Christian leader?**

- above reproach (v 2)
- the husband of one wife (v 2, 12)
- sober-minded (v 2)
- self-controlled (v 2)

- respectable (v 2)
- hospitable (v 2)
- able to teach (v 2)
- not a drunkard / not addicted to much wine (v 3, 8)
- not violent but gentle (v 3)
- not quarrelsome (v 3)
- not a lover of money / not greedy for dishonest gain (v 3, 8)
- manages his own household well, with all dignity keeping his children submissive (v 4, 12)
- not a recent convert (v 6)
- well thought of by outsiders (v 7)
- dignified (v 8)
- not double-tongued (v 8)
- holds the mystery of faith with a clear conscience (v 9)
- tested (before being allowed to serve as a deacon, v 10)
- their wives must be dignified, not slanderers, but sober-minded, faithful in all things (v 11)

- **How do these compare to the characteristics of some of the leaders we read about in the media?**
  Answers will vary. It will be easy to start complaining about world leaders who do not live up to these characteristics, so encourage your group to also think of some examples of good leadership, even if those leaders are not Christians.

Explore More

- ***Read Proverbs 31:4-5. How was a leader's relationship with alcohol spelled out by King Lemuel's mother?***
  King Lemuel's mother warns him that when a leader has been drinking, he may forget what has been decided and go against the very people he is meant to protect. Notice that a leader doesn't have to be drunk to make bad alcohol-influenced decisions.

---

9. **An overseer "must not be a recent convert" (v 6) and "must be well thought of by outsiders" (v 7). What reasons does Paul give for this?**
   Verse 6: Oversight in the church must not come from recent converts because of the ever-ready capacity of leaders to become proud or "puffed up with conceit". Worldly leadership is often about place, significance, importance and power. Christian leadership is about service and caring, sacrificial love. A recent convert may not yet see the difference and, full of worldly thinking, fall prey to the same "condemnation of the devil".
   Verse 7: To be "well thought of by outsiders" means that non-Christians who know the overseer should be able to provide good testimony of him. If he has given outsiders no reason to think well of him, or (worse) every reason to think poorly of him, he may well fall into such disgrace that he is trapped by the devil and brought down.

- **Can you think of any other reasons why these two characteristics matter?**
  An overseer of God's household will bear a disproportionate amount of the persecution that comes to all who desire to live for Christ Jesus. A mature faith will help them to cope with this in a wise manner. Also, since the church aims to share the gospel with those who do not yet know Christ, that message must not be stained by a leader who is thought of poorly by those the church is trying to reach.

10. **Christian leadership is "a noble task" (v 1) but also a hard one. What could you do a) this week and b) this month to help the pastor of your church or the leader of your group to be a faithful leader?**
    Encourage your group to come up with specific answers to these questions and to write them down, as this makes it far more likely that they will then put them into action. One possible answer is to pray for your leaders, but if a group member chooses this option, encourage them to also think of how they will let their leader know when they will be praying and what they will be praying for.

11. **Both lists address the dangers of abusing speech, alcohol and money. Which of these is most likely to be a temptation for you, whether you are a leader or not? How will you handle that temptation this week?**
    If your group is large or people will find it hard to answer this in front of everyone else, consider pairing people and asking them to share an answer with their partner. Encourage partners to pray for each other during the coming week.

3

Godliness Training

1 Timothy 3:14 - 6:2

The Big Idea

The essence of godliness is not our behaviour but our relationship with God. One way that we honour God is by honouring other people.

Summary

Chapter 3:14-16 is the centre-point of 1 Timothy—not just in terms of being in the middle of the letter, but more importantly, in being at the centre of the argument of the letter and the reason for

Paul writing to Timothy at all.

Timothy was Paul's protégé, holding the fort for him while he delayed his coming. The letter sets out the moral imperative of how one "ought" to behave, specifically in the household of God, the church. The appropriate behaviour of a household member is the outworking of the truth of the great confession of the secret of godliness. This secret of godliness is spelt out in the six propositions in 3:16.

Taking these propositions in turn, we find that the central truths of godliness are quite different from people's expectations of morality. Christian piety or religion is different from other religions in that it is not about ceremony, ritual, tradition or "worship". Rather, true religion is the relationship with God, through Jesus the Christ, that issues forth not only in reconciling forgiveness of our sins but also in the changed life of loving God.

This change of behaviour is so great that sometimes we limit the word "godliness" to the behaviour of God's people—that is, their morality. But the opposite of biblical godliness is not so much ungodliness as godlessness. For the essence of godliness is not our behaviour but our relationship with God.

Paul continues to warn Timothy about false messengers. In the face of their false message, Timothy is to "put these things before the brothers" (4:6). He is directed to train himself in accordance with or relation to godliness. This is not a command to practise Christian behaviour but to commit himself to the gospel and its teaching, in contrast to secular and silly myths (4:7). It is embracing what God has done for us by Christ, as announced to us in the gospel. It results in the behaviour one ought to have in the household of God, which Paul is explaining in the rest of the letter.

The household of God comprises many different relationships. In chapter 5, Paul instructs Timothy, and us, how believers ought to behave in this family. The topic that unites this part of Paul's instructions to Timothy is that of "honour". Be it the widow, the elder or the master, Christians must honour others. In turn, this way of relating to others brings honour to God.

Optional Extra

Imagine describing what a Christian is to someone who has never come across the term. Can you come up with a brief description that doesn't include anything about what Christians *do* or *don't* do?

Don't spend too long on this activity. The aim is to show us how easily we fall into the trap of seeing Christian living in terms of rules that tell us what we can and can't do. But Paul is going to show us in this part of 1 Timothy that the essence of godliness is our *relationship* with God through Christ.

Guidance for Questions

1. **Choose three words to describe Jesus. Why did you pick those three?**

   This question will give group members something to compare with Paul's list of six things about Christ in 3:16. Their answers may also show

how each person feels about Jesus—and the depth of their understanding of who he is and what he has done for us. This can be helpful knowledge when you are thinking through how best to help each member of your group to grow.

2. **In question 1 you thought of three words to describe Jesus. In 3:16, what six things does Paul tell us about Jesus, and what do you think each one means?**
   - *"He was manifested in the flesh"*—This is often understood to refer to the incarnation, when God became flesh. But it is much more likely to refer to Jesus' bodily resurrection, when he appeared (was manifested) repeatedly to the disciples.
   - *"Vindicated by the Spirit"*—After the resurrection, it was in the outpouring of the Spirit that Jesus was finally seen to be both Lord and Christ (Acts 2:33-36). His identity, and his place at God's right hand, were proved (vindicated) by the Holy Spirit.
   - *"Seen by angels"*—Angels were the first witnesses of the resurrection, greeting the women and disciples at Jesus' tomb and declaring that he was not there but risen.
   - *"Proclaimed among the nations"*—The preaching of the gospel to the nations (or Gentiles) was the reason Paul was "appointed a preacher and an apostle" (1 Timothy 2:7). Likewise, the apostle Peter was shown by God that the good news about Jesus was for Gentiles as well as Jews (Acts 11:1-18).
   - *"Believed on in the world"*—For 21st-century people, it is no big deal that Jesus would be "believed on in the world". But in the first century, and for a Jewish man like Paul, the idea that the Jewish Messiah would be believed in throughout the world was wonderful and slightly extraordinary. But that was what Paul was seeing all around him—as the gospel went out to the nations, all manner of people were coming to faith in Jesus.
   - *"Taken up in glory"*—Jesus now sits at God's right hand in all power and glory, from where he will one day return to judge the living and the dead.

3. **What reason does Paul give for some "departing from the faith" (4:1), and how do they hear these wrong teachings (4:2)?**

Those who depart from the faith will do so by "devoting themselves to deceitful spirits and teachings of demons" (v 1). It would be foolish to think that all teaching and ideas are only human, and thus ignore the possibility that they may have a supernatural source.

Even though this wrong teaching is supernatural, it comes via humans—"through the insincerity of liars whose consciences are seared" (v 2). This harsh description of the false teachers is nevertheless true because they *are* liars—the children of the father of lies (John 8:44). What they speak is untrue. And more than untrue, it is *intentionally* untrue because of their insincerity.

4. **Verse 3 gives an example of false teaching. What was being taught, and how does Paul counter that in verses 3-5?**
   There are two examples of false teaching in verse 3—teaching that marriage is forbidden, and insisting that people don't eat certain foods.

   Paul reminds us that "everything created by God is good" (v 4). This means that all of God's creative pleasures are to be received with thanksgiving (v 3).

   NOTE: The doctrine of creation is one of the distinctives of the Bible. It teaches that God is not part of creation but that he created it for his good purposes—and so the physical world is good, and humans are responsible for its use and care. Ascetics say the world is evil; materialists say the world is accidental—neither see it as good, nor do they give humans spiritual responsibility for it.

Explore More

- ***Read Colossians 2:20-23. What rules had the Colossian Christians made for themselves?***
  The Colossian Christians had made rules about things they were not to handle, taste or touch. (NOTE: The Greek word translated as "handle" in verse 21 is also used for kindling a fire or lighting a lamp. So, to "handle" something probably means to pick it up and do something with it, whereas "touch" means touching it with a finger.)

- ***Can you think of modern-day equivalents?***
  Modern-day equivalents could be rules against smoking, drinking alcohol or reading secular books. None of these prohibitions make us right with God—only faith in Christ can save us.

  NOTE on verse 10: While we're not directly discussing 4:10 in this study, someone in your group may ask about the difficult ending ("the Saviour of all people, especially of those who believe"). Verse 10 is a battleground text which people argue over to support their own beliefs about salvation. Some try to use this verse to claim that all people are saved. However, "all people" cannot mean that everyone will be saved, as that contradicts clear teaching from elsewhere in Scripture (John 14:6; Acts 4:12; 1 Timothy 2:5). So Paul adds the caveat "especially of those who believe" lest it be thought that all would be saved. Jesus is the one and only Saviour of all people, but only those who trust him are saved by him.

---

5. **Which words in 4:13, 15 and 16 show how committed Timothy needs to be to the ministry of the**

word of God? What will be the result (v 15, 16)?

Timothy needs to be *devoted* (v 13, 15) and *persistent* (v 16). He also needs to keep *practising* (v 15).

The result will be that everyone will see Timothy's progress (v 15), and that both Timothy and those who listen to him will be saved (v 16).

Verse 15 is one of those bitter-sweet messages for Bible teachers: sweet in that we do not have to have "arrived" before we can minister the word of God—for Timothy was not to show his arrival but his progress. It's bitter in that we can never rest on our laurels—for Timothy had to continue to show his progress. By reading the Scriptures and by encouraging and teaching with patient persistence, Timothy will be bringing the gospel of salvation in Christ Jesus to bear on himself and his hearers.

6. **How might this apply to your life this week:**

- **in your church relationships?**
- **with those outside of church?**

Timothy was in the difficult position of being a young man who had been commanded (v 11) to teach those older than him. They could easily despise him because of his youth (v 12). So Paul called Timothy to set an example to his elders of godly behaviour in the household of God (3:15). Timothy was to set an example "in speech, in conduct, in love, in faith, in purity". Encourage your group members to think of at least one situation this week where they can choose to avoid ungodly behaviour and instead say or do something that befits a member of God's household. Such opportunities might come up at church, in your small group or other church events; and at work, in the home, at the school gate, while driving, etc.

7. **When Paul wrote this letter, Timothy was a young man. How was he to treat those in the church family: older men, younger men, older women and younger women?**

Timothy is to treat...

- older men like fathers, and not rebuke them (meaning he must respect the age or seniority of the older men and not rebuke them in the same way he would a younger man).
- younger men like brothers (meaning he is not to look down on them or lord it over them).
- older women like mothers (meaning he is to respect their seniority and encourage them with affection).
- younger women like sisters, in all purity. (This is because sexual drive could easily come into play here, so Timothy must treat younger women with absolute purity.)

In every case, we are to relate to people as relatives—as members of the same loving family.

8. **The question of honouring widows takes the next 14 verses (v 3-16). What are the four kinds of widows**

Paul refers to, and who should take care of them?

NOTE: Not all widows are the same. So in his directions, Paul distinguishes between different widows and different circumstances of life. But his concern is always the same: that Christians honour widows appropriately, and that Christian widows serve Christ appropriately.

- **v 4**

  Older widows who have relatives to support them. Their biological family should be looking after them (v 4, 16). This pleases God (v 4).

- **v 5**

  Older God-fearing widows who have no relatives to support them. The church is to "enrol" such widows so that they are provided for (v 9). By only supporting this kind of widow, the church is protected from being over-burdened (v 16).

- **v 6**

  Older self-indulgent widows ("self-indulgent" means to "live excessively in luxury", so these widows live for the pleasures of money rather than depending on God in prayer, as the faithful widows do in verse 5). Paul's concern is to protect the church from being burdened (v 16). The church did not have the capacity to provide for all widows, and the priority had to be the genuinely needy widows of the household of faith who had no other means of support. So Paul gives no instruction that the church should support these unfaithful widows. However, if such a widow also has relatives, then their family does have responsibility for them (v 8). To fail to do so would be to be "worse than an unbeliever" (v 8).

- **v 11**

  Younger widows are at least under 60 years of age (v 9) and possibly also still of childbearing age (v 14). These younger widows are not to be "enrolled" (v 11). They are to take responsibility to care for themselves. This is because of the spiritual damage done to younger widows when the church takes responsibility for them. Paul sees problems with their passions (v 11) and their idleness (v 13). These are not simply theoretical problems but real pastoral issues, as some of the flock "have already strayed after Satan" (v 15). Younger widows also have a responsibility to care for any relatives who are widows (v 16).

9. **How are elders to be honoured (5:18-19)?**

   Elders are to be paid (v 18) and protected (v 19).

   Paid: "You shall not muzzle an ox when it treads out the grain" is a quote from Deuteronomy 25:4. In 1 Corinthians 9, Paul explains that God's concern about the ox extends to his concern that those who labour in the gospel should reasonably expect to be paid for their labour (1 Corinthians 9:1-14). The second quote is from Luke 10:7, where Jesus teaches the same thing when he says, "The labourer deserves his wages". Note that Paul may be using "elders" differently from how you use this term in your church. In verse 17 he refers to those who "rule well" and who "labour in preaching and teaching", so these are church leaders. If your own church has a group of men serving as "elders", Paul isn't necessarily saying that they should all be paid financially for serving in this way (although we should still honour them).

Protected: Elders are to receive protection from false accusations. Paul is alluding to the Old Testament rule on the inadmissibility of the evidence of only one witness (Deuteronomy 19:15). Leaders are easy targets, so the minimum standards of evidence must be strictly kept if justice is to be done.

- **How and why should slaves honour their masters (6:1-2)?**

  Slaves are to "regard their own masters as worthy of all honour" (v 1). If their masters are fellow Christians, slaves must not use that as an excuse to be disrespectful; instead they are to serve their masters even better (v 2). When we bear the name of Christ, people judge our Lord by our behaviour. So, when Christian slaves honour and serve their masters, it prevents God's name, and Christian teaching, from being reviled (v 1; see also Titus 2:9-10). Instead, believing masters, who are loved brothers in Christ, will benefit from being served well (v 2).

  NOTE: Ever since the early 19th century, slavery has been viewed as unthinkable, unconscionable and unmentionable. Sadly, this evil is still practised around the world today. Yet the slavery of Paul's day was considerably more diverse than the 18th-century African slave trade. In the Roman world, Paul's point was that slaves should "regard [their] own masters as worthy of all honour". This means working for them not as men-pleasers, who only work hard when watched by the master, but genuinely from the heart (Colossians 3:22).

10. **1 Timothy 5:19 outlines how to protect elders from false accusations. How was Timothy to deal with true accusations (v 20)?**

    When someone "persists in sin" (v 20), it becomes clear to all that the accusation against them is true. Timothy's task with sinners is to rebuke them—to expose the error and convict the sinner of their guilt. The command to do this in the presence of all indicates that this is not some private sin. The reason for the rebuke to be in public is "so that the rest may stand in fear" (v 20). The aim of confronting sinners is always repentance and restoration, not condemnation and self-satisfaction (Galatians 6:1-5). When Jesus speaks of treating the sinner as a Gentile and tax collector, he is not speaking as a Pharisee, who would have nothing to do with the sinners, but as the

Saviour who would eat and drink as a friend with sinners and tax collectors—and lay down his life to save us (Matthew 9:10-13; 11:19; 21:31-32; Romans 5:6-8).

11. **In 1 Timothy 5:1 – 6:2, Paul shows us that we honour God by honouring others. How will the motivation of bringing glory to God make a difference to how you honour others this week?**

Encourage group members to choose at least one way they can intentionally honour someone this week. This could be someone from Paul's list (widows, elders, masters) but doesn't have to be. Perhaps you could agree to ask each other next week how you have got on.

4

The Great Gain of Godliness

1 Timothy 6:2-21

The Big Idea

"There is great gain in godliness with contentment" (v 6), so avoid the things associated with godlessness and instead fight the good fight of the faith.

Summary

Timothy has been entrusted with a great responsibility (1 Timothy 1:18) and the whole letter instructs him in how, as one who professes the secret of godliness, he is to behave in God's household. His task has been to silence opponents by laying the truth before the church. And this guarding of the deposit involves "avoiding the irreverent babble" (see 1:4; 4:7; 2 Timothy 2:16) and "contradictions of what is falsely called 'knowledge'" (1 Timothy 6:20). God wants people to come to the knowledge of the truth (2:4), but sadly the false teachers and their followers do not know the way to the truth (2 Timothy 3:7).

This last chapter of 1 Timothy unpacks this further for Timothy.

Behaviour that befits membership of God's household comes from the distinctive truth of godliness (1 Timothy 3:15-16). The distinctive character of this godliness is seen in the conflict with false teachers—with "anyone [who] teaches a different doctrine" (6:3). This is where the letter commenced in 1:3, and continued with Paul's charge to wage the good warfare against such false teaching and teachers (1:18). Now it comes to the particulars of their behaviour that differ so markedly from godliness.

The different doctrine "does not agree with" two things—it does not agree with "the sound words of our Lord Jesus Christ" (these are the sound or healthy words of Jesus himself); and the false teachers do not agree with "the teaching that accords with godliness" (for the message of the gospel religion is unique). Godliness is all about what God has done for us in Christ Jesus, but the alternatives are all about what we have to do as we seek to be acceptable to God.

Paul's first defence against those who think godliness is a means to gain surprises most people. For instead of denying the error, he seems to agree with it: "There is great gain in godliness with contentment" (1 Timothy 6:6). Paul is agreeing that godliness is great gain. This is consistent with his earlier teaching that godliness is of value in every way—for the present life and for the life to come (4:8). The key lies in contentment: in being content with reality. Though the gospel is about this world—Jesus appearing in it bringing the grace of God to it—yet it is primarily and fundamentally about the world to come.

Mention of the appearing of our Lord Jesus Christ in 1 Timothy 6:14 provokes in Paul an outpouring of praise to God in another doxology (6:15-16). It is to this one and only God, who will display his Son again in his appearing, to whom Paul ascribes "honour and eternal dominion" (6:16). For whom else would you want to be ruler for ever?

At the end of 1 Timothy, Paul sums up his challenge with the command, "O Timothy, guard the deposit entrusted to you". So much of the letter has been about Timothy's role in challenging error and maintaining truth that it is a fitting summary. Paul again warns of the false teaching and its dreadful consequences, which need to be avoided—for maintaining the truth requires exposing the errors. And he concludes with a fitting and much-needed prayer for his protégé as Timothy faces the joys and challenges of gospel ministry—"Grace be with you".

Optional Extra

Give each group member a sheet of paper and ask them to design a logo to illustrate 1 Timothy 6:12—"Fight the good fight of the faith".

Guidance for Questions

1. **Who is the most contented person you know? What do you think is the secret of their contentment?**

   This opening question introduces the subject of contentment, which Paul addresses in 1 Timothy 6:6.

2. **What happens to the person who "teaches a different doctrine" (v 3-4)?**

   They become puffed up with conceit (v 4).

   Although they are teachers, they "understand nothing" (v 4). (Paul says the same thing about the false teachers in 1 Timothy 1:7.) They crave controversy and love to quarrel about words.

- **What is the result of this false teaching (v 4-5)?**

  Envy, dissension, slander, evil suspicions and constant friction. The people who follow such false teaching are "depraved in mind and deprived of the truth" (v 5). They think that godliness is a means to an end, and so aim for such "godliness" purely for what they think they will get out of it (v 5).

3. **In verse 5, those who listen to false teaching are described as "imagining that godliness is a means of gain". But in verse 6, Paul states that "there is great gain in godliness". How can both of these be true?**

The contrast here is one of motivation. The false teachers are telling people that they will gain wealth if they follow their (wrong) teaching (which is often about following religious rules, such as we saw in 4:3). Today, we would call this the "prosperity gospel", where preachers declare God's desire to make Christians wealthy—especially if we are generous with our money, in particular to the preacher's ministry. Such preachers promise that the good things of eternal life will arrive now, in this lifetime, in this world. So the motivation to live in a particular way (pushed by the false teachers as godliness, but not true godliness) is to gain riches now.

But for biblical Christians, whose motivation is to honour and serve the Lord, there truly is great gain in godliness. This is consistent with Paul's earlier teaching that godliness is of value in every way—for the present life and for the life to come (4:8).

4. **A desire to be richer (whether in money, possessions or experiences) breeds discontent. What strong words and phrases does Paul use to show what happens when we approach life in this way (v 9-10)?**
   - v 9: Senseless and harmful desires, ruin, destruction
   - v 10: A root of all kinds of evils, pierced with many pangs

- **What terrible result has Paul seen in the lives of some people in the church (v 10)?**

  They have "wandered away from the faith".

Explore More

- ***Read 2 Corinthians 8:1-9. How was the church in Macedonia in many ways the opposite of what Paul warns against in 1 Timothy 6:9-10?***

  Despite their own affliction and poverty (v 2), they overflowed in joyful generosity. They did not want more for themselves; instead, they wanted to give away more (v 3-4).

- ***What is the key to this kind of generous contentment, does 2 Corinthians 8:9 suggest?***

  Knowing and experiencing true riches—all that we have in Christ, sharing with him his eternal life and his status with his Father. When we know all that we have in him, we seek to follow his example—and he gave up the wealth of heaven to know the poverty of the cross, so that he could give us eternal riches.

---

5. **Do you find it easy to agree with Paul that "if we have food and clothing, with these we will be content"? Why / why not?**
   This question will begin to tease out what we really mean by "contentment".

- **Do you find it easier to be content when you have much or when you have little? (See Paul's view of contentment in Philippians 4:10-13.)**
  To some, this may seem a strange question, but Paul clearly saw the need to be able to be content with a lot as well as with little. Having little can lead to jealousy or grasping for more. Having a lot does not reduce jealousy and grasping but increases the opportunity for us to exercise our sinfulness. And even those of us with a lot can usually find someone with more to be jealous of!

6. **How does living a godly life model contentment to those around you? What impact do you think this will have on other Christians and on those who are not Christians?**
   This is an opportunity to apply Paul's teaching directly to our own lives, and also to consider how the way we show contentment makes a difference to those around us.

7. **What is Timothy told to pursue in verse 11?**
   Timothy is to pursue the alternatives to the love of money (v 10). He is to pursue "righteousness, godliness, faith, love, steadfastness, gentleness" (v 11). This is a short list—not by any means a comprehensive list—of the desires and aspirations to be pursued not only by Timothy but also by anyone who would be a man or woman of God.

8. **Back in verses 9-10, we were warned about the danger of riches. What kind of riches are we encouraged to pursue instead in verses 17-19?**
   - v 17: Riches from God (who provides every good thing we enjoy)
   - v 18: Doing good / good works; being generous and ready to share what God has given us

9. **Would someone who knows you describe you as rich in wealth, or in good works and generosity (or neither)?**

- **What can you change this week to be the second kind of rich man or woman?**
  Answers will vary, but encourage each group member to write down at least one thing, even if they don't feel able to share it with the group.

- **How has this passage motivated you to be that person?**
  Ensure your group thinks about positive motivations, as well as the (very real) negative warnings.

10. **In verses 11-12 Timothy is told to *pursue*, to *fight* and to *take hold*. These are all very active terms. Do you think you are this active in living for Christ? Is there something more you could be doing?**
If group members struggle to answer this, you could pick out some of the characteristics Paul lists in verse 11, such as faith or steadfastness, and ask them how they can actively grow in these characteristics. There is a balance here between pursuing/fighting (implying we are fully committed to living for Christ) and recognising that it is the Spirit working within us who shapes us to be more like Jesus. So alongside the things we plan to do, we need to pray for the Spirit's help and that all the glory will go to God.

5

Do Not Be Ashamed

2 Timothy 1:1 - 2:13

The Big Idea

Christian ministry is ordinary Christians faithfully proclaiming the powerful gospel of God. It involves hard work and inevitable suffering, but it is worth it because the gospel is powerful, and Christ has risen, and eternal life is secured.

Summary

Christians today are proud of the apostles and their imprisonments. But I wonder if we would have been so proud had we been living in apostolic times. It is this embarrassment or shame that is in sight when we approach Paul's second letter to Timothy.

Paul was in prison when he wrote 2 Timothy. He was fast becoming a family embarrassment. He admitted—and actually boasted about—his many "imprisonments, with countless beatings" (2 Corinthians 11:23). Yet this time this imprisonment looked final (2 Timothy 4:8).

Paul reminds Timothy to "fan into flame the gift of God" (v 6). Timothy is about to be charged with an extraordinary task that needs all the supernatural strength that comes from God. A "spirit ... of power and love and self-control" is needed for his (and our) ministry (v 7).

The challenge of the passage is in verse 8: "Do not be ashamed of the testimony about our Lord, nor of me his prisoner" (v 8). It would be easy for Timothy to be ashamed of his mentor and his message. They always seem to wind up in defeat and disaster. But when he called people to be his disciples, Jesus warned that on the day of judgment he would be ashamed of anybody who is ashamed of him and his words (Mark 8:38). Jesus has destroyed death and brought immortal life through the gospel (2 Timothy 1:10)—so there must be no shame about living and teaching it, nor of those who do that (like Paul). Timothy is not to be ashamed as Paul is not ashamed (v 12) and Onesiphorus is not ashamed (v 16).

God's call and recruitment of Timothy into his plans and purposes was not a matter of merit, but neither was it a matter of punishment. It was all a matter of grace—mercy, generosity—on God's part (v 9). And the gospel message must be passed on—Timothy was to entrust it to faithful men who, because of their faithfulness, would be able or worthy to teach it to others (2:2).

The task of being teachers of the gospel involves suffering (2:3). In three quickly stated illustrations, Paul outlines the internal discipline of the soldier, the athlete and the farmer (2:4-6). Each has to put their own pleasure and comfort aside as they undertake their task faithfully.

This chapter is one of the great statements on the nature of Christian ministry. It is not about institutions, positions, ordinations, techniques or ecclesiastical haberdashery. It is about Christians faithfully teaching the powerful word of God in the context of normal human hard work, and the inevitability of suffering as Christ's servants.

Optional Extra

Ask the best baker in your group to make something particularly lovely (e.g. some brownies or cookies). To begin with, take out just one portion of the baking, and tell your group it will be given to the person who is willing to do the most push-ups/star-jumps, etc. (You choose the nature of the challenge based on the general fitness levels of your group!) Once the person in question has performed the challenge, give them the food (and then share the rest of the food around—and if there are complaints about this, point out that this is grace!) The purpose is to make the point that we are willing to undergo hardship for what we value most—and in this passage, Paul is showing Timothy that the gospel, and proclaiming the gospel, are of infinite value—and therefore worth suffering for, rather than being ashamed of.

Guidance for Questions

1. **When you're with non-Christian friends or family, how do you feel about sharing the gospel?**

- **How would you define "Christian ministry"? Who does it, and what does it involve?**

  Encourage honest answers to these questions, especially the first. There is no need to guide the group towards "correct" answers at this stage—these questions will be picked up again when you reach questions 6-7 and questions 11-12.

2. **What do these verses tell us about...**

- **Paul?**
  We are reminded that Paul is an apostle, as you will have thought about in session 1 (v 1). Paul was in chains in prison when he wrote 2 Timothy (v 8, 16). (This was not his first imprisonment. It would be closer to the truth to say he was in chains again.) This imprisonment looked final. No release was in sight. Paul—who was not a man to dramatise his situation—was writing about dying (4:8). Moreover, Paul has been abandoned by some (though not all) of his friends and partners in ministry (1:15). He is not only chained in prison—he is, increasingly, on his own.

- **Timothy?**
  Timothy's sincere faith did not commence with him but with his grandmother first and then also his mother (1:5). It was Timothy's "sincere" faith (v 5)—but his mother and grandmother, Eunice and Lois, had the same faith that he grew to share. We do not hear of his father. Paul is certain that the faith of his mother and grandmother "dwells in you as well" (v 5).

- **the relationship between them?**
  Paul addressed his letter to "Timothy my beloved child" (1:2). Timothy was not Paul's physical son—he was his son in the faith (1 Timothy 1:2)—but the relationship between the two men was as deep and profound as if they had been related. Paul remembers Timothy constantly in his prayers (2 Timothy 1:3). He longs to see him again and recalls Timothy's tears (presumably over their separation). Such a reunion would fill Paul with joy. Indeed, he wants to see Timothy so that—even though, or especially, because he is in prison—he may be filled with joy (v 4).

3. **What does Paul tell Timothy to do in verse 6?**
   Paul reminds him to "fan into flame the gift of God, which is in you through the laying on of my hands" (v 6). This does not necessarily mean that the flame was flickering or dying. Timothy is about to be charged with an extraordinary task that needs all the supernatural strength that comes from God. The nature of Timothy's gift is not explained here, but 1 Timothy 4:14 talks about his gift of teaching the word.

- **What does verse 7 show us this will look like?**
  God has given "us" a spirit or disposition not of fear but of power, love and self-control. The reasons Paul raises this will become clear in the next verse, but here we are considering these attitudes.
  - "Fear" is something we all understand, and it would limit Timothy's ability to use his gift in the situation Paul is writing about. There is no suggestion that Timothy is timid and needs some bolstering up for the task. The task Paul has in mind is a fearful one. The alternative and antidote to natural fearfulness is the triad of traits that finish the verse.

- "Power" is the ability to get things done. The particular power that we Christians have is the power to endure our cross. We are not magicians who do miracles but cross-bearers who endure suffering and shame. That is what verse 9 will go on to discuss.
- "Love" is necessary, as it is critical in this ministry to think of others rather than self. To lay down your life for others and their salvation is the essence of love.
- "Self-control" is necessary if we are to live not by our passions and emotions but by the wisdom of knowing what is right and doing it.

4. What does Paul tell Timothy to do (and not to do) in verse 8?

He is to "share in suffering for the gospel by the power of God". It is not an invitation to masochism—to some perverse pleasure in suffering. It is precisely suffering for Jesus and the gospel that Paul talked about, and lived out, and is now writing about.

Negatively, Timothy must not be ashamed: neither of the testimony of our Lord nor of its messenger. When he called people to be his disciples, Jesus warned that on the day of judgment he would be ashamed of anybody who is ashamed of him and his words (Mark 8:38).

- **How would verses 9-14 encourage Timothy to obey Paul's commands in verse 8?**
  - v 9: It is God "who saved us and called us to a holy calling, not because of our works but because of his own purpose". God is at work in the world, saving people and calling them to a different, holy, eternal life (1 Timothy 6:12; Romans 8:28-30). Paul and Timothy are in God's plans and purposes. This is not because of their works (religious or moral) but because of God's own sovereign purpose. God's call and recruitment of Timothy into his plans and purposes was all a matter of grace—mercy, generosity—on God's part. Suffering for the gospel is a privilege, for it is part of being allowed to be part of the way God is at work in his world.
  - v 10-12: Jesus is the risen Lord of heaven and earth, the conqueror of death, who has brought life and immortality to light (v 10). And he is the one who is able to bring us into that immortality with him (v 12). This opens a whole new future to us—one of hope and eternity. The very telling of this message transforms the lives of the hearers. How could anyone dare to be, or want to be, ashamed of it?! And that is also why Timothy is not to be ashamed of Paul, the Lord's prisoner. For it was to this gospel that Paul "was appointed a preacher and apostle and teacher" (v 11), and it was for this gospel ministry that Paul suffered his imprisonment (v 12).
  - v 14: The Holy Spirit has been given to him and dwells within him; and so he will be able to "guard the good deposit entrusted to you".

God has not left him alone in this difficult task.

Explore More

- ***Read 2 Corinthians 11:23-29; Philippians 1:12-18; Romans 1:14-17. What do these passages tell us about what Paul experienced in the course of his ministry?***
  His list of experiences in 2 Corinthians 11 shows us just how hard ministry was for Paul. It led to his imprisonment on several occasions (including the one during which he wrote to the Philippians) before the one referenced in 2 Timothy.
- ***What do they tell us about what Paul prioritised during his ministry?***
  - *The health of the churches he had founded (2 Corinthians 11:28-29)*
  - *The proclamation of the gospel, no matter what that meant for his own well-being or reputation (Philippians 1:17-18), because it was able to save anyone (Romans 1:16-17). Paul considered himself bound to, or in debt to, both Jews and Gentiles until he had told them the gospel (Romans 1:14-15).*

---

5. What positive examples of obeying verse 8, and contrasting examples of disobeying, do we see in verses 15-18?

This little episode in Paul's imprisonment reveals starkly contrasting examples both of shame and of being unashamed. Everyone in Asia (Turkey) deserted Paul in his time of trial. Most, like Phygelus and Hermogenes, were ashamed of Christ's prisoner. But one man, Onesiphorus, was unlike the rest. He refreshed Paul and was not ashamed of Paul's chains (v 16).

6. In what contexts is it most tempting to be "ashamed" of the gospel, or of other Christians?

Ensure the conversation remains focused on your own contexts (perhaps the workplace, or sports club, or with wider family), rather than contexts where others may be ashamed (e.g. in countries where Christians are persecuted). Make sure you discuss the second part of the question too—it is all too easy to be ashamed about other Christians who are willing to be mocked in order to speak out or stand firm.

7. What would it look like to follow Paul's "pattern" (v 13) in those situations? How would the truths of verses 9-12 motivate and empower us?

This question is designed to encourage you to think about what a positive "not ashamed" gospel witness will look like. Make sure you are specific in discussing the situations you identified in the previous question, and in question 1.

8. Why does that make the command of 2:2 crucial for the church?

Because it ensured that Paul's ministry would not terminate with the first generation of Christians. This verse mentions four generations of gospel ministers. Paul and Timothy belong to the first two, and then the faithful men who teach others make up generations three and four. Here is the plan for the future—not the establishment of an institution but the faithful transmission of a message. It was to be set before and entrusted to others—Paul had had it entrusted to him, and as he entrusted it to Timothy (1:12, 18), so Timothy was to entrust it to others. The choice of whom to entrust with this ministry was not based on a person's skill or ability or giftedness in teaching but their faithfulness—that they would loyally teach what had been entrusted to them.

9. To what three jobs does Paul compare the task of gospel teaching and gospel sharing (v 3-6)?

- Soldier (v 3)
- Athlete (v 5)
- Farmer (v 6)

- **What does Paul want to show us about Christian ministry?**
  The struggle Paul has in mind here is not the external suffering caused by persecution but the internal discipline necessary to be a good minister. The soldier, the athlete and the farmer all have to put their own pleasure and comfort aside as they undertake their task faithfully. The soldier must avoid civilian distractions, the athlete illegal shortcuts and the farmer laziness. So, a good servant of Christ Jesus will keep his eyes on pleasing the Lord Jesus and not get distracted by the things of this life.

10. How would Paul, "bound with chains as a criminal" (v 9) and Timothy, facing the struggles of Christian ministry, be encouraged by the truths of...

- **verse 8?**
  In the area of sharing in suffering as a good soldier, it is especially critical to understand life in the light of Jesus "risen from the dead". It is by his resurrection appearing that Jesus has abolished death and brought life and immortality to light. His conquest over sin and death and all the forces of evil is a great comfort to those who are now enduring suffering in his name.

- **verses 11b-13?**
  Paul makes four statements here:
  - "If we have died with [Christ] we will also live with him." Here is the basic idea of becoming a Christian: he redeemed us by dying as our representative and substitute, and calls us to lose our lives for his sake and the gospel in order to gain the life he gives (Mark 8:35).
  - But in this world, that new life will be persecuted, so there is the great encouragement of 2 Timothy 2:12, that "if we endure, we will also reign with him". Jesus "endured the cross, despising the shame, and is seated at the right hand of the throne of God" (Hebrews 12:2).
  - However, as Jesus himself pointed

out, "If we deny him, he will also deny us" (2 Timothy 2:12). He called upon the crowds to deny themselves, take up their cross and follow him—but he warned that "whoever is ashamed of me and of my words in this adulterous and sinful generation, of him will the Son of Man also be ashamed when he comes in the glory of his Father with the holy angels" (Mark 8:38).

- The fourth is the strangest statement: "If we are faithless, he remains faithful—for he cannot deny himself" (2 Timothy 2:13). Most likely it is speaking of the temporary faithlessness reflected in every sin of a believer, and yet Christ remains true to his word and rescues those who have momentarily lost confidence in Christ. However we understand verse 13, the emphasis is upon the consistent faithfulness of Christ—for he cannot deny himself.

- **How would those truths motivate them to "endure everything for the sake of the elect" (v 10)?**
  God's chosen people needed to hear the gospel in order to be saved, and to be ministered to with the gospel as they continued to walk in faith. And that faith brought eternal glory with Christ, reigning with him (v 10-12). Any hardship was worth going through in order to secure that. If that meant prison, so be it.

11. **Having read Paul's message to Timothy from 1:1 – 2:13, what words would you use to describe Christian ministry?**
    Link back to question 1 here. Hopefully, your group will come up with words such as suffering, hardship, discipline, gospel, teaching, privilege, blessing, grace, calling.

12. **What happens to our own ministry if we forget...**
    - **that ministry involves suffering?**
      We will stop making the efforts required, because we will be surprised by how hard it is.

    - **that ministry requires self-discipline?**
      We will never get round to actually proactively pursuing ministry opportunities, or we will find ourselves very easily deflected into other pursuits and pleasures, and again never quite get round to doing the ministry God sets before us.

    - **that Christ has risen, is guarding us, and will bring his people to life with him?**
      We will grow demoralised. Ministry will not seem worth the cost.

    - **that the Spirit gives us power, love and self-control?**
      We will grow despondent or (perhaps worse) proud and self-reliant. Remembering that these things come from the Spirit makes us prayerfully dependent on him in all our ministry.

6

Work and Life in the Last Days

2 Timothy 2:14 - 3:17

The Big Idea

The normal Christian life involves facing difficulty and persecution in a world that is in love with itself. But as we continue in what we believe, and live by God's word and speak out God's word, we will be useful servants of our Master.

Summary

Words are important for Christian teachers, who are responsible to teach the word of God. At the same time, instead of listening to God's word, sinful people are quite capable of quarrelling and fighting over words.

The work of Christian ministry (of all kinds) is described as "rightly handling the word of truth" (2:15). Rather than quarrelling over words or using words to gossip (v 14, 16, 23), Timothy is to speak the truth that God's word expresses and reveals. And he is to live in such a way that his actions match those words (v 22-26). It is so important that we exemplify the message that we are teaching.

And the importance of rightly handling the word of truth is emphasised by understanding the times that Timothy and we live in: "In the last days there will come times of difficulty". The last days will be difficult because sinful people are still going to be sinful, and opposition to God and his people is only going to grow (v 2). Verse 5 is the key text of verses 1-9. Having spoken of the evil of the people of the last days in verses 2-4, and before going on to talk of their false religion and its demise in verses 6-9, Paul states that these people will be "having the appearance of godliness, but denying its power". Here is the real problem: people oppose the truth of the gospel while practising the externals of Christianity! So Timothy must "avoid such people" (v 5). Perhaps Hymenaeus and Philetus are prime examples of those who have the form of religion but deny its power, as they upset the faith of some by their irreverent babble (v 17-18).

2 Timothy 3:12 is one of the more extraordinary statements about the normal Christian life: "All who desire to live a godly life in Christ Jesus will be persecuted". To live by, and proclaim, the name of Jesus in evil times will mean at least that you become unpopular, if not that you are persecuted outright. So the great command of Paul to his protégé is to "continue" in what he has learned—in particular in the Scriptures (3:14-15). For the Scriptures will make him wise for salvation in Christ Jesus and equip him, as a "man of God", for every good work that God has in store for him (3:15-17).

Optional Extra

Ask each member of your group to bring in something from their home which is worth a reasonable amount and is of personal value to them. Put the items on a table and have group members guess what belongs to whom. Then ask each group member to talk about their own item, and how it is valuable, perhaps financially but, more importantly, personally. This links with verses 20-22 and the idea that, as Christians, we want to live and work and speak in ways that make us "useful to the Master".

Guidance for Questions

1. **If you had to sum up your expectations for your Christian life in a ten-word sentence, what would you say?**
   You will return to this in question 11.

2. **In what ways are Timothy and the "faithful men" he works with (the "them" of verse 14) to use their words (v 14-15, 24-25)?**
   - v 14: Timothy is to "charge them before God not to quarrel about words". This is a matter of great seriousness. They are going to be held accountable for it by God himself.
   - v 15: They must "rightly [handle] the word of truth". This is a great statement of the work of all Christian ministry, from teaching our children at home to preaching to thousands in a stadium. "Do your best" in this verse translates the Greek command to "make every effort" or "to pursue with zeal and fervour". They must teach the truth of God's word accurately and correctly, for God's word is "the word of truth", which must be taught in such a way that it expresses and reveals that word. Their words must make the truth that God intends to communicate in his word clear to the hearer.
   - v 25: They are to correct those who are opposed to them (as they correctly teach the word), but with gentleness, as this combination of truth and kindness is the means most likely to bring about repentance.

3. **What does Paul warn them about (v 16-18)?**
   They must "avoid irreverent babble" (v 16), and Paul also warns them about the danger of "[swerving] from the truth" (v 18), as two men, Hymenaeus and Philetus, who had presumably previously professed faith in Christ, have done. To modern ears, "irreverent babble" sounds like swearing or gossip, but the profanity Paul has in mind here is the denial of the gospel truth concerning the resurrection (v 18).

- **Why (v 14b, 16, 18)?**
   - v 14b: Because it does no good—in fact, it ruins people. People who are opposed or indifferent to the truth will dispute and argue about the words in which truth is expressed in order not to have to listen and obey. There are those who would prefer to deconstruct the cry of "Fire!" rather than leave

the burning building which will soon entomb them.

- v 16: Quarrelling about God's truth leads to "more and more ungodliness". Remember, the word "godliness" does not equal goodliness but rather, God-orientation. So here, ungodliness is godlessness rather than immorality. It's the denial of the great secret of godliness—the gospel (1 Timothy 3:16). This is the "ruin" of verse 14b: people led further and further away from God and a right relationship with him. And this can spread like "gangrene"—once that starts, it is very hard to stop, and is life-threatening.
- v 18: It "shakes the faith of some"—"shakes" could mean destruction here. This underlines the seriousness of quarrelling about or denying, instead of obeying, the word of truth.

- **How do verses 20-22 motivate Timothy in this kind of life and work?**

Because this is the kind of Christian who is "useful to the Master". Someone who does not follow or associate with false teaching, but instead rightly handles the word of truth, is like an "honourable" vessel, approved by and useful to God.

4. In verses 22-26, what is the link between the way Timothy is to live and the words he is to say, do you think?

Timothy is told to flee youthful passions. The paragraph goes on to indicate what these youthful passions are, for he is to "have nothing to do with foolish, ignorant controversies". Few people are more argumentative than the testosterone-fuelled youth who wants to win arguments! But "the Lord's servant must not be quarrelsome" (v 24). It is so important that Timothy and we not only teach the truth but also teach it truthfully—that we exemplify the message that we are teaching.

It is not by force of personality or cleverness of argument that we will be able to persuade our opponents into repentance. Rather, it is God who may, in his mercy, grant repentance to somebody. And this God-inspired repentance is the path to someone coming to a knowledge of the truth.

5. In what situations—with Christians as well as in the wider world—do you find it easy to misuse your words?

Along with these verses in 2 Timothy, you may find it helpful to read out James 1:19 and Ephesians 4:29. Think about times when, and people about which, you can be critical, negative or caustic, or engage in gossip; times when, instead of listening well, you are too quick to speak; situations in which you could speak about Bible truth, but choose to allow conversation to remain ascriptural (or, worse, unscriptural).

- **How could you "rightly handle the word of truth" in those contexts?**

This is an opportunity for you to

consider positively the way in which you can (as appropriate) either let what you say be guided by what Scripture says, or actually speak words of truth from Scripture to others. God does not want us merely to keep quiet when we might naturally otherwise have been critical, or joined in with gossip, or affirmed ungodly behaviour, etc. He calls us to speak positively and speak gospel in those moments.

6. **What should Timothy expect as he seeks to live as a Christian?**

- **v 1**

  Times of difficulty

- **v 2-4**

  People to remain sinful. So as the gospel is preached, we are always to expect opposition, hostility, false teachers, false rumours and ridicule. Paul lists here some of the ways that people's sin will manifest itself. Notice the expressions of our loves mentioned in verses 2 and 4: naturally we are lovers of self, lovers of money and lovers of pleasure rather than lovers of God. And between these expressions of our loves comes a long list of the activities that characterise those who love self, money, and pleasure above any love of God. This is not to say that all people will only always be evil all the time, but that the character of this age, even with Christ on the heavenly throne, will be godless and wicked.

- **v 6-7**

  Some people will use religion and religious knowledge in order to enslave or take advantage of others. Here are people who oppose the truth of the gospel while practising the externals of Christianity! They are religious charlatans: men of corrupt mind and faith who oppose the truth and the true prophets of God; men who entice the unstable and weak with learning that is based in ignorance, taking captives into their ways. They are always claiming to be "learning" but they never come to any conclusion (v 7). They seem very open-minded but are closed to accepting the truth.

  NOTE: This passage is not saying that all women are weak and burdened with sins and passion. But it is saying that some are, and that such women are very vulnerable to these religious charlatans.

7. **What should Timothy do in response to these people (v 5)?**

   "Avoid such people."

- **What do you think this means in practice?**
  - Timothy is not to ignore ungodly people or never spend time with them (otherwise he would not be following the model of Jesus, nor of Paul!). But he is to be careful about following such people. It is far too easy to start out seeking to be a witness of the truth to those who are rejecting Christ, and end up living and speaking very much like them. Timothy (and we) must avoid

that, and that may sometimes mean avoiding those people altogether.

- We are specifically not to fellowship with those who maintain the form and appearance of godliness while denying its truth and power—for their false teaching and ways not only upset the faith of some but also spread like gangrene, killing and putrefying all who come into contact with them (1 Corinthians 5:9-13). This may even mean finding a new church where the word of truth is rightly handled.

Explore More

- ***Scan-read Exodus 7:8 – 8:19. What were Jannes and Jambres able to do when Aaron's staff turned into a serpent... the Nile turned to blood... and frogs infested the country (7:11-12, 22; 8:7)?***
  They were able, through their own powers, to ape each miracle.
- ***What were they able to do when the dust became gnats (8:18)?***
  Nothing!
- ***What did they therefore realise (v 19)?***
  That this was God's doing, and that their power could not compare to the God-given power of Moses and Aaron.
- ***How does this show the truth of Paul's claim in 2 Timothy 3:9?***
  Eventually, those who seek to oppose God and the truth of the gospel, though they may be able to give an appearance of power and success for a while, will be revealed for what they are—charlatans, leading people into folly, who fail to deliver what they promised. (NOTE: In some cases, this takes years or even decades.)
- ***How have you seen this to be the case in your own life as a Christian?***
  Some of your group may be able to share examples from their own experience, or that of people they know. Don't let your study go off on a tangent at this point—if you are short of time, skip this question.

---

8. How should he respond?

- **v 10-11: By following...**
  Paul's example. He taught the truth in the context of a life conducted with purpose, trusting God and loving others with resolute endurance. Timothy has seen how to live, shown to him by his great mentor.
- **v 12-13: By remembering...**
  That those "who desire to live a godly life ... will be persecuted" (v 12), even as those who oppose the gospel while pretending to teach it thrive or grow in influence (v 13). Paul is writing of all Christians when he speaks of those "who desire to live a godly life in Christ Jesus". Living a godly life in Christ is not an optional extra for the superspiritual. This is the normal Christian experience. It is the God-related life of the Christian, as opposed to the godless

life. People are rarely persecuted for "goodliness". But proclaiming and living the gospel of Jesus always provokes a reaction. To live by and proclaim the name of Jesus in evil times will make you at least unpopular, if not lead to outright persecution. Verse 12 is not saying that Christians will be persecuted every minute of every day, but that at some time or other they will be persecuted. It is not saying that they *may* be persecuted but that they *will* be.

- **v 14-17: By continuing...**
  To hold to the truth that he learned from his childhood, in the Scriptures, which teach the truth about how to be saved ("in Christ Jesus"), and to continue to believe those Scriptures.

  NOTE: The Greek word for "continue" translates as "remain" or "stay"—don't move. In the face of any and all opposition, Christians are to hold fast, be steadfast, persevere, and endure suffering by the power of God.

9. **Why should the Bible be at the centre of every Christian's life (v 15-17)?**
   Scripture is so powerful because "all Scripture is breathed out by God" (3:16). The Scriptures are not simply the writings of men, nor the researched discovery or inquiry of humans (2 Peter 1:20-21). The Scriptures are God speaking. Scripture benefits believing readers by...
   - teaching them, because the Bible shows us the truth and the right way to walk in life.
   - reproving them, because the Bible tells us when we go wrong and challenges our errors.
   - correcting them, because the Bible explains how to get back on track and put things right again.
   - training them in righteousness, because the Bible tells us and shows us the pathways of right living.

10. **How can you follow Paul's instructions in verses 10-17, and help one another to do this?**
    Think about how your conversations with each other, your activities together, and what you do for one another, is helping (or hindering) each of you in...
    - providing good models of faithful living to one another.
    - accepting persecution as normal (instead of doing virtually anything to avoid it, and excusing each other for that).
    - keeping the Scriptures central to your lives, and helping one another to read them to remember that you are saved in Christ, but also to teach, reprove, correct and train each other.

11. **If you now had to sum up your expectations for your Christian life in a ten-word sentence, what would you say?**
    Hopefully now the passage will reshape the answers given for question 1.

7

I Charge You...

2 Timothy 4:1-22

The Big Idea

Faithful ministers are those who preach God's word clearly and continually, however unpopular that is. It is what we should celebrate in our pastors and seek to do in our own ministries, so that we, like Paul, can one day look back on our lives with satisfaction.

Summary

Paul reaches his final great challenge: "I charge you…" (4:1). First, Paul reminds Timothy that Jesus is going to judge the living and the dead. He is the one to whom Timothy is answerable, for through his "appearing" (his resurrection), he is in charge of the world as King.

The charge is simple: "Preach the word" (v 2). He is to proclaim the gospel. "Preach" does not mean stand in a pulpit, but rather, "proclaim" or "declare". He is to do it with constancy—even when it confronts others—and continually.

It will not be popular, however, for people will give up on sound teaching (v 3), and when this happens, people do not turn to no teaching but to false teaching that supports their "own passions". Timothy, however, is to preach the word and so fulfil the ministry he has been given (v 5).

Timothy's commission to preach the word has two time considerations relevant to it. First, the last days are times when people won't listen anymore. Second, Paul is about to depart the scene (v 6-8). That Paul is on the final lap, if not the home straight, is clear from the three statements in verse 7. He has kept faith in finishing the course of ministry that he was given to accomplish (as Timothy must do), and he is looking forward to the crown laid up for him—a permanent crown given by the risen Jesus (v 8).

In some ways, we can feel that the letter finishes in something of an anticlimax. But verses 9-21 remind us that Paul was a real person: that he enjoyed loving fellowship with others, and that his priority was to keep going in ministry to the end (v 13). And they reveal how Paul had been accused and faced a court alone (v 14-16); but that Jesus had been with him so that he could proclaim the truth, and he had survived the hearing (v 17—it is not clear whether "the lion's mouth" is referring to literal lions, or a terrifying trial).

The final greeting (v 22) wishes Timothy personally the Lord's presence and, alongside all who read this letter, God's grace (the last word "you" is plural). Timothy and all God's people need this grace or favour of God as we live for Christ in the last days.

Optional Extra

In pairs, write a job description for "the perfect pastor". (Depending on your group, you can do this in a humorous or a serious way.) After question 6 or 11, return to your description and compare it with the job spec that this passage (or, if you have time, the whole of 1 & 2 Timothy) would direct you towards.

Guidance for Questions

1. **What makes someone a good church leader?**
   Allow all kinds of answers at this point, though make very sure this does not turn into an opportunity to talk about ways in which group members think your own church leader(s) should change.

2. **How does Paul underline the seriousness of "the charge" he is giving Timothy here (v 1)?**
   God is witnessing the charge that Paul is declaring to Timothy; and not only God but also Christ Jesus—and Jesus is going to judge the living and the dead. He is the one to whom Timothy is answerable, for "we must all appear before the judgment seat of Christ, so that each one may receive what is due for what he has done in the body, whether good or evil" (2 Corinthians 5:10). Timothy's salvation was assured, but it was important that he did "not ... receive the grace of God in vain" (2 Corinthians 6:1).

   Paul also invokes Jesus' "appearing and his kingdom". The "appearing" of Jesus refers to his resurrection, by which established his present kingdom. He is not only going to judge the living and the dead but also now is in charge of the world as the risen King.

3. **In verses 2 and 5, Paul tells Timothy how he must "preach the word". For each subordinate command, think through what this would have required of Timothy in his everyday ministry.**

- **Be ready in season and out of season**
  Preaching the gospel is something he is to do constantly, whether it is convenient or inconvenient, in any moment of life. It is not simply when the preacher feels like it or has set aside time for it. Now is the day of salvation, so now is the season to preach the word.

- **Reprove, rebuke and exhort**
  Timothy needs to be prepared for his preaching to confront his hearers. The word "reprove" is the verb form of the word "reproof" (3:16). The concept of "rebuking and exhorting" is similar to the Scriptures' correcting and training. The proclamation of the gospel always calls for repentance, so by nature it is confrontational, because it is declaring that the hearer is going the wrong direction. Timothy needs to be prepared to teach in this way—for his preaching to risk unpopularity in order for it to do what the word of God is designed to do.

- **With complete patience and teaching**
  He will need to keep going, to persist. Preaching quick one-time sermons is not the method to adopt in a world that doesn't want to listen. Preaching the word is not a one-off activity but something that takes time for people to hear and understand, let alone respond to in repentance and belief.

- **Be sober-minded**
  "Sober" is the opposite of drunk because it means to be serious, sane, well-balanced, sensible and self-controlled. Proclaiming the word of God is not a trivial and lighthearted activity. To rightly handle the word of truth (2:15) requires serious, self-controlled, considered hard work.

- **Endure suffering**
  Suffering is inevitable in a fallen world. But the suffering Paul is writing about is the cost of godliness (3:12). Timothy is to proclaim the very heart of godliness—the gospel of the risen Lord Jesus. He will suffer for it—and he must accept this, and continue in this.

- **Do the work of an evangelist**
  Paul is not adding an extra task to Timothy's job description here. It is not as if he is to do an evangelist's work in addition to his work of preaching the word. These are not mutually exclusive ministries—the apostle Paul, for example, did them all. The command to "preach the word" is the challenge to do the task of the evangelist—for preaching the word is what evangelists do. Preaching the word is by definition evangelistic, and true evangelism always involves proclaiming the gospel—preaching the word.

  NOTE: The only person called "the evangelist" in the New Testament is Philip. His work is described in Acts 8, where, together with all those scattered by Saul's persecution, he went about preaching the gospel (Acts 8:4). His evangelism among the Samaritans, with the Ethiopian eunuch and in all the towns from Azotus to Caesarea, is described as preaching the gospel (Acts 8:12, 35, 40).

- **Fulfil your ministry**
  This is Timothy's task—what modern people might call his "success criterion". He is to proclaim the word, and he is to get on with it!

4. **Why will this task be difficult (v 3-4)?**
   Because "people will not endure sound teaching" (v 3). Paul has already written about the difficulty of the last days (3:1-9). Now he speaks of how that time will see hostility to the word of God. People will lose patience with sound teaching. When people give up on sound teaching, they do not turn to no teaching but to false teaching. So the people to whom Paul refers are described as "having itching ears [and so] they will accumulate for themselves teachers to suit their own passions". *Choose your own teacher* is widely

practised in the globalised Christianity of the internet. This puts pressure upon preachers to become celebrity preachers by diminishing or, worse, distorting the content of God's word. Sadly, they are the very ones who become most popular, for they say what people want to hear. They are not "rightly handling the word of truth" (2:15). The choice of teachers should be based on faithfulness to the message but is often, as Paul indicates, based on suiting the listener's "own passions". And so as Timothy (and every faithful gospel minister) preaches the word, he will find that people "will turn away from listening to the truth and wander off into myths" (v 4).

5. **"A faithful pastor will not often be a popular one." To what extent is this true, do you think?**
   Certainly 2 Timothy (and the rest of the New Testament) suggests this is largely true. That is not to say that anyone who pastors a large church, or who is asked to write columns in the secular media, is suspect. But it is to say that numbers and, far less, being respected by the culture are not measurements of gospel faithfulness or pastoral success. A faithful pastor, particularly in a post-Christian culture such as the West today, will cause offence, put people off (because they do not wish to listen to the truth), and face unpopularity. This is no excuse for a pastor to make himself unpopular! But it is to accept that being faithful will sometimes inevitably bring criticism and accusation, and these should not be considered reasons to change the message.

6. **To what extent does your church value in your pastor(s) the characteristics Paul called for in Timothy?**
   Again, do not let this turn into a discussion of how your pastor(s) can and should do better (unless they are not preaching the word!). Instead, focus on your own expectations and (perhaps subconscious) "success criteria" for your church leaders. It is very easy, in every kind of church, to prize some kind of appearance or approach or entertainment factor above core faithfulness to the word.

- **How can you show your pastor(s) your appreciation for the ways in which they fulfil this ministry?**
  Make sure you are practical, and perhaps agree to ask one another in a month's time whether you have put your ideas into practice.

7. **How does Paul view his life, and his death?**
   Paul metaphorically describes the certainty of his death by using the image of the outpouring of a drink offering. (In Old Testament Israel, an offering of wine or water was poured on top of an animal sacrifice presented to God.) He is not saying his death will be immediate, but the cup has been tipped and the drink is now pouring out. He then says the

same thing more literally, though still talking in terms of "departure" rather than simply death. As a believer in the resurrection, death is only a departure.

That Paul is on the final lap, if not the home straight, is clear from the three statements in verse 7. The "fight" is not a militaristic term, but more of a gymnastic struggle. Both this image and the next, about finishing the race, are really illustrating the basic statement: "I have kept the faith". This is not so much about fighting or running, though both require effort—the point he is making is that he has finished, and finished well, for he has kept the faith, meaning, "I have remained faithful". This is what life is about for Paul—staying faithful to Christ, whatever the cost.

Since Paul has done this, he is looking forward to the athlete's victory symbol—a crown laid up for him that is not perishable but permanent. And Paul is certain it is coming, because it is to be awarded by "the Lord, the righteous judge". Who better to give the crown of righteousness than the righteous judge?

8. How does this add gravity and urgency to his "charge" to Timothy?

Since Paul is about to depart the scene, Timothy (and others) will need to continue the work of faithful gospel ministry, preaching the word and raising up the next generation of word-proclaimers as they do so. Paul will not be around to continue to encourage Timothy by his letters and his example.

9. What insights do these verses give us into...

- **Paul's friendships?**

  His loving fellowship with others shows that his ministry was not a solo effort but one with many colleagues and protégés.

- **Paul's hardships?**
  - *Desertion:* Demas having left because he was "in love with this present world" (v 10) is a very sad statement, but Paul had also had to say goodbye to good friends (v 10-12, 20).
  - *Physical hardships:* He would need a cloak before winter (v 13).
  - *Accusation and trial:* Verses 14-18 tell of an attack on him and the strains of appearing in court. We know nothing of Paul's enemy Alexander the coppersmith other than that he did Paul great harm (v 14), sufficient for Paul to warn Timothy to "beware of him yourself, for he strongly opposed our message" (v 15). Paul also outlines the very sad fact that "at my first defence no one came to stand by me, but all deserted me" (v 16).

- **Paul's priorities?**

  He wants Mark to come, for he is "useful to me for ministry" (v 11); he desires his books and parchments so he can keep reading and working (v 13). He is a great example to those who are tiring. His main encouragement from his trial is that, in the Lord's strength, the Gentiles heard the gospel message (v 17). Do not miss that Paul's priority remains ministry, even as he is in captivity and anticipating death.

10. **How should Paul's example here shape the way we view the whole concept of "retirement"?**
    Paul's retirement plan was not to enjoy a superannuation income in a luxury villa overlooking the sea. His ultimate retirement plan was to receive the athlete's victory symbol—a crown laid up for him. Until he died and went to be with his Lord, he had work to do. Retirement is therefore, in a sense, not an option for a Christian. We may decide it is prudent to retire from our paid work, but we must never retire from our gospel ministry or step back from our commitment to Christ's mission. Paul did not seek a few years at the end of his life in which to relax, see the world, and let others do the hard work. Neither should we.

11. **How should Paul's example here shape our view of what matters most in life?**
    By reminding us that on the last day, what will matter is whether we kept the faith—were we faithful to Christ in discharging the ministry he had entrusted to us, preaching the word where and when we could in a way that was clear and faithful. We are all too easily deflected into other matters—homes, families, holidays, possessions, experiences—that matter far less.

Explore More

- ***Scan-read the whole of 1 and 2 Timothy. What does Paul remind Timothy about...***
- ***who Jesus is and what we enjoy through faith in him?***
- ***what Christian ministry involves?***
- ***what life will be like for the committed Christian?***

  You could split your group into three, and ask each sub-group to keep one of these questions in mind as they scan-read the letters, writing down verses that speak to that question as they read through.

12. **Through 1 and 2 Timothy, in what ways has the Spirit of "power and love and self-control" (2 Timothy 1:7) been encouraging and challenging you to guard the gospel deposit that has been entrusted to you (v 14)?**
    Ask your group to write down two or three answers to this question individually, before you share them together. Of course, you will all have different answers. If you think it would help your group, you could task each group member with following up in a month the person sitting to their right, by asking them how they have been getting on with living out what they wrote down in answer to this question.